Guardians of the Virtual Realm

From Protection to Penetration: Navigating Cybersecurity and Ethical Hacking Techniques

Harper Grey

Table of Contents

INTRODUCTION

The 21st century is an interconnected digital age where information is easily shared and technology permeates almost every part of our lives. As such, protecting our digital lives is more important than ever. This book, "Guardians of the Virtual Realm: From Protection to Penetration - Navigating Cybersecurity and Ethical Hacking Techniques," explores the complex realms of ethical hacking and cybersecurity, illuminating the ever-changing terrain of ethical penetration and digital defense.

The difficulty facing individuals and enterprises in this era of data breaches, ransomware attacks, and constantly changing cyber threats is how to safeguard private information, intellectual property, and sensitive data from the continuous assault of cybercriminals. Once pushed to the periphery of IT issues, cybersecurity is now a top priority for corporations, governments, and private citizens alike.

The mysterious subject of ethical hacking, sometimes called "white hat" hacking, is at the center of this digital battleground. Here, knowledgeable individuals use their skills to outsmart cybercriminals by behaving and thinking like them. They explore the shadowy reaches of the internet, looking for and testing weaknesses before malicious actors can take advantage of them. To safeguard, defend, and secure our digital world is their mission.

This book takes readers on a thorough exploration of the field of cybersecurity and provides them with a broad understanding of both the attacks that pose a significant risk and the defenses available against them. Every chapter serves as a stepping stone toward digital resilience and competency, covering everything from cybersecurity and ethical hacking principles to the complexities of network defense, web application security, and new developments in the field.

Whether you are an experienced cybersecurity professional seeking to broaden your knowledge or a curious novice keen to learn the basics, this book will provide you with the understanding, resources, and methods required to navigate the ever-changing cybersecurity environment successfully. Together, we will delve into the subtleties of ethical hacking, translate cyberthreat language, and establish a solid cybersecurity plan.

In this book, we set out on a journey from protection to penetration, ensuring that you, the reader, are ready to face the opportunities and challenges that lie ahead in cybersecurity and ethical hacking. The digital frontier is both the battlefield and the frontier of progress.

Are you prepared to start this fascinating and essential journey? Time to start the trip.

CHAPTER I

Understanding Cybersecurity Fundamentals

What is cybersecurity?

In the digital age, where technology permeates every facet of our lives, the term "cybersecurity" has assumed monumental significance. It has become the guardian at the gate of our increasingly interconnected world, protecting us from a host of digital threats that have the potential to disrupt, damage, and even devastate. Cybersecurity is the collective armor we wear to shield our data, systems, and digital identities from an array of malicious actors and cyberattacks.

At its core, cybersecurity is the practice of safeguarding digital assets against unauthorized access, manipulation, or destruction. It encompasses various technologies, processes, and practices designed to defend our digital infrastructure. These assets can include personal information, financial data, intellectual property, government secrets, and the critical infrastructure that underpins essential services like electricity, water supply, and transportation.

Cybersecurity is the cornerstone of trust in the digital realm, where information flows ceaselessly. It ensures that our online interactions remain secure, our data remains confidential, and our transactions remain free from tampering or theft. Without robust cybersecurity measures in place, the very foundations of our digital society would crumble.

One of the central challenges that cybersecurity addresses is the ceaseless evolution of cyber threats. As technology advances, so too do the tactics employed by malicious actors. Cybercriminals constantly seek new vulnerabilities to exploit, whether through malware, phishing attacks, or advanced persistent threats. Thus, cybersecurity is not a static concept but a dynamic, ever- evolving field that demands constant vigilance and adaptation.

To combat these threats, cybersecurity employs a multifaceted approach. It begins with risk assessment, a process for identifying potential vulnerabilities and threats. Once these vulnerabilities are known, protective measures are implemented to mitigate risks. These measures may include firewalls, intrusion detection systems, encryption, and security policies.

An integral part of cybersecurity is also incident response planning. No system is entirely impervious to attack, and when breaches occur, a well-defined plan ensures that damage is minimized, and recovery is swift. Incident response teams work tirelessly to investigate breaches, contain the damage, and restore normal operations.

Additionally, cybersecurity is concerned with user education and awareness. Many cyberattacks, such as phishing, prey on human error. Thus, educating users about safe online practices and recognizing potential threats is crucial to a comprehensive cybersecurity strategy.

Furthermore, cybersecurity extends its reach to the rapidly growing Internet of Things (IoT) landscape. As more devices become connected to the internet, from smart thermostats to industrial control systems, the attack surface expands exponentially. Ensuring that these devices are secure and do not pose vulnerabilities is a pressing concern in the field of cybersecurity.

Government agencies also play a vital role in cybersecurity. They formulate and enforce regulations that dictate how organizations should protect sensitive data. Moreover, they often engage in cybersecurity initiatives to protect national interests and critical infrastructure.

Cybersecurity is not solely the responsibility of governments or corporations; it's a shared endeavor. Each individual interacting with the digital realm has a role in cybersecurity. This includes using strong, unique passwords, updating software, and being vigilant for suspicious activity. In this sense, cybersecurity is a collective responsibility that relies on the cooperation and vigilance of all digital citizens.

The consequences of failing to address cybersecurity adequately can be severe. Financial losses, identity theft, and reputational harm are all possible outcomes of data breaches. For organizations, the fallout from a cyberattack can be catastrophic, leading to massive financial losses and, in some cases, bankruptcy. On a larger scale, cyberattacks on critical infrastructure can disrupt essential services, posing threats to public safety and national security.

In conclusion, cybersecurity is the digital shield that guards our interconnected world. It encompasses many technologies and practices that protect our digital assets from ever-evolving cyber threats. It is not just a concern for governments and corporations but a shared responsibility that requires the active participation of every individual. As technology continues to advance, so too must our commitment to cybersecurity. In a world where our lives are increasingly intertwined with the digital realm, the importance of cybersecurity cannot be overstated. It is the bulwark that ensures our digital society remains secure and resilient, and it is a field that will continue to evolve as we navigate the challenges of an interconnected world.

The evolution of cybersecurity

The evolution of cybersecurity is a remarkable journey through the annals of digital history, a narrative shaped by the relentless march of technology and the ceaseless ingenuity of those who would protect our digital realms. From the rudimentary security measures of the earliest computer systems to the complex, AI-driven defenses of today, the story of cybersecurity is one of adaptation, innovation, and an unending battle against an ever-evolving array of threats.

In the early days of computing, cybersecurity was practically nonexistent. The digital landscape was a vast, uncharted wilderness where the pioneers of technology, oblivious to the dangers that lurked, sought to explore and exploit the potential of these newfound electronic machines. Security, if considered at all, was relegated to rudimentary methods, such as physical locks on computer rooms.

It was in the 1970s that the need for more robust cybersecurity measures began to emerge. The proliferation of computer networks, including ARPANET (a precursor to the modern internet), raised concerns about data integrity and confidentiality. This era witnessed the birth of encryption standards, with the Data Encryption Standard (DES) being one of the first widely adopted cryptographic protocols. DES laid the foundation for securing data in transit, but it also foreshadowed the relentless arms race between cybercriminals and cybersecurity experts, as its encryption was eventually broken through brute force attacks.

The 1980s marked a pivotal moment in the evolution of cybersecurity with the emergence of computer viruses.

The advent of personal computers, interconnected through bulletin board systems (BBS), provided fertile ground for these malicious programs to spread. The infamous "Morris Worm" of 1988, created by Robert Tappan Morris, became one of the earliest instances of a worm spreading across the nascent internet. This incident underscored the need for better security practices, leading to the development of the Computer Emergency Response Team (CERT) by Carnegie Mellon University in 1988, a pioneering effort in incident response and coordination.

As the 1990s dawned, the internet's expansion accelerated, introducing new security challenges. Firewalls, intrusion detection systems (or IDS), and antivirus software became essential tools for protecting computer networks. However, the threat landscape continued to evolve. The late 1990s saw the rise of distributed denial of service (DDoS) attacks, where a network of compromised computers (a botnet) inundated targeted systems with traffic, rendering them inaccessible. This marked a shift from simple attacks to more coordinated and destructive campaigns.

The new millennium brought with it a heightened sense of urgency regarding cybersecurity. High-profile attacks, like the ILOVEYOU worm and the Code Red worm, demonstrated the global reach and devastating impact that cyber threats could have. In response, governments and organizations worldwide began to invest heavily in cybersecurity. Legislative acts, like the USA PATRIOT Act in the United States, aimed to bolster national security by enhancing cybersecurity measures.

The mid-2000s witnessed the proliferation of mobile devices and the advent of cloud computing, expanding the attack surface for cybercriminals. Mobile malware and data breaches became prevalent concerns, prompting the development of mobile security solutions and strict regulations for data protection, like the General Data Protection Regulation (GDPR) of European Union.

As technology continued to advance, so did the sophistication of cyber threats. Advanced Persistent Threats (APTs), state-sponsored cyber espionage, and cyber warfare became realities. Stuxnet, a computer worm discovered in 2010, marked a new era in cyber warfare by explicitly targeting industrial control systems, effectively blurring the line between physical and digital security.

An unprecedented period of data breaches began in the 2010s, with corporations such as Equifax, Yahoo, and Target being among the most prominent victims. Millions of people's personal information was compromised by these breaches, underscoring the significance of data confidentiality and security. Cybersecurity evolved to encompass network and endpoint security, data protection, threat intelligence, and security awareness training.

Amidst these challenges, a new paradigm emerged— cyber resilience. Recognizing that no system could be entirely impervious to attacks, organizations focused on their ability to withstand and recover from cyber incidents. Incident response plans and disaster recovery strategies became integral components of cybersecurity efforts.

The advent of the 2020s brought with it a new set of cybersecurity challenges. The COVID-19 pandemic accelerated digital transformation, with remote work and online collaboration becoming the norm. Cybercriminals exploited the chaos and uncertainty, launching phishing campaigns, ransomware attacks, and exploiting vulnerabilities in remote work setups.

Today, the cybersecurity landscape is characterized by rapid technological advancements and an ever-evolving threat landscape. Cybersecurity professionals and malicious actors leverage artificial intelligence and machine learning, creating a dynamic battlefield where algorithms and automated tools are used to detect and combat threats.

The evolution of cybersecurity continues to be shaped by the push and pull between those who seek to defend digital assets and those who aim to exploit vulnerabilities. It's a relentless pursuit of innovation on both sides, with ethical hackers and security researchers playing a crucial role in identifying and reducing vulnerabilities before they can be exploited maliciously.

Looking to the future, cybersecurity will remain a paramount concern as technology continues to advance. Quantum computing, for example, poses both a threat and an opportunity, as it has the potential to break current encryption standards while also enabling new cryptographic techniques that are quantum-resistant.

In conclusion, the evolution of cybersecurity is a testament to human ingenuity and adaptability in the face of a rapidly changing digital landscape. From the early days of rudimentary security to today's sophisticated defenses and threats, the journey of cybersecurity reflects our ongoing commitment to securing the digital realm. As we move forward, the lessons learned from the past will continue to guide us, reminding us that the battle for digital security never truly ends.

Key concepts: Threats, vulnerabilities, and risks

Three key ideas—threats, vulnerabilities, and risks— underlie the entire field of cybersecurity in today's intricate environment. Comprehending these ideas is crucial for anybody attempting to manage the constantly changing landscape of digital security. Threats represent the arsenal of potential dangers lurking in the digital shadows, vulnerabilities are the weak points within systems and processes that adversaries exploit, and risks are the consequences that materialize when threats meet vulnerabilities. In this section, we delve deep into these key concepts, unraveling their significance, interplay, and the critical role they play in shaping cybersecurity strategies.

At the heart of cybersecurity lies the notion of threats. These are the adversaries, hazards, or malicious entities that seek to compromise digital assets' integrity, confidentiality, or availability. Threats come in a staggering array of forms, each with its own motivations, techniques, and potential for harm.

One of the most prevalent threats in the digital realm is malware. For malicious software, malware encompasses viruses, worms, Trojans, ransomware, and other insidious programs. These digital parasites infect systems, steal data, disrupt operations, or extort ransoms, often with devastating consequences.

Phishing attacks represent another significant threat. Cybercriminals use deceptive emails, messages, or websites to trick individuals into divulging sensitive data like passwords, credit card numbers, or personal identification. Social engineering, a psychological manipulation technique, is frequently employed in phishing campaigns, making them highly effective and challenging to detect.

Distributed Denial of Service (DDoS) attacks are yet another example. In these attacks, a network of compromised computers, known as a botnet, floods a target system with an overwhelming traffic volume, rendering it inaccessible. DDoS attacks can paralyze critical online services, wreaking havoc on businesses and individuals.

Moreover, advanced threats like Advanced Persistent Threats (APTs) and state-sponsored cyberattacks have risen in prominence. These are typically well-funded and highly organized operations, often with political or economic motivations. They can infiltrate networks, remain undetected for extended periods, and exfiltrate sensitive data or manipulate critical systems.

In essence, the landscape of digital threats is continually evolving, with new tactics and techniques emerging regularly. As such, cybersecurity professionals must remain vigilant, adapting their strategies to counter the ever-changing threat landscape.

While threats represent digital adversaries, vulnerabilities are the Achilles' heel of systems, applications, and processes. Vulnerabilities are weaknesses or flaws that threats can exploit to obtain unauthorized access or cause harm. They are the proverbial chinks in the armor, and identifying and addressing them is at the core of effective cybersecurity.

Vulnerabilities can manifest in various forms. They may be found in software code, hardware configurations, human behavior, or even in organizational policies and procedures. For instance, software vulnerabilities can arise from coding errors, known as software bugs or flaws. These errors can create openings for attackers to exploit, potentially leading to data breaches or system compromise.

Operating systems and software applications, being complex and constantly evolving, are fertile grounds for vulnerabilities. Software updates and patches are regularly released to address known vulnerabilities, making timely patch management a critical aspect of cybersecurity hygiene.

Human behavior can also introduce vulnerabilities. Weak or reused passwords, careless handling of sensitive information, and falling victim to social engineering schemes are examples of how human actions can expose vulnerabilities within an organization.

Organizational vulnerabilities may stem from lax security policies, insufficient employee training, or inadequate incident response plans. Without a robust cybersecurity posture, an organization may inadvertently create opportunities for threats to exploit.

It is worth noting that not all vulnerabilities result from negligence or poor design. Zero-day vulnerabilities, for instance, are flaws in systems or software that are unknown to the vendor or developers. Threat actors often seek and exploit these vulnerabilities before patching them, making them particularly dangerous.

The intersection of threats and vulnerabilities gives rise to risks. Risks represent the potential harm or damage that can occur when a threat successfully exploits a vulnerability. It is the quantification of the likelihood and impact of an adverse event taking place.

Cyber risks come in various forms, from financial losses and reputational damage to legal consequences and operational disruptions. When a threat, such as a malware infection, successfully exploits a vulnerability, it can lead to the loss of sensitive data, financial theft, or a breach of confidentiality.

For organizations, risks extend beyond immediate financial losses. Reputational damage can erode trust with customers and partners, potentially leading to a loss of business. Legal risks, including regulatory fines for data breaches or non-compliance with cybersecurity standards, can result in significant financial penalties.

Moreover, risks in the digital realm can have cascading effects. An attack on critical infrastructure, like the power grids or healthcare systems, can disrupt essential services, impacting public safety and national security.

Understanding and managing risks is a foundational aspect of cybersecurity. Risk assessments, often conducted using methodologies like FAIR (Factor Analysis of Information Risk), help organizations quantify and prioritize risks. Risk mitigation strategies involve reducing vulnerabilities, enhancing threat detection and response capabilities, and developing resilience to minimize the impact of potential incidents.

In conclusion, the concepts of threats, vulnerabilities, and risks form the bedrock of cybersecurity. Threats represent the ever-evolving arsenal of digital adversaries, while vulnerabilities are the weaknesses that adversaries exploit. When threats successfully exploit vulnerabilities, risks materialize, potentially resulting in financial losses, reputational damage, and operational disruptions. Effective cybersecurity hinges on identifying and addressing vulnerabilities, implementing robust threat defenses, and quantifying and mitigating risks. Mastering these key concepts in the dynamic digital landscape is essential for safeguarding digital assets and maintaining digital resilience.

Cybersecurity framework and best practices

In an era marked by the relentless march of technology and an ever-expanding digital frontier, the importance of cybersecurity has never been more pronounced. Organizations and individuals alike face an evolving landscape of digital threats that can disrupt, damage, and devastate. Cybersecurity frameworks and best practices have emerged as critical tools to navigate this complex terrain, offering structured guidance to fortify digital defenses, protect sensitive data, and safeguard the digital realm.

A cybersecurity framework is a structured approach to managing and mitigating cybersecurity risks. It is a comprehensive guide outlining essential processes, policies, and practices necessary to protect against cyber threats. While various frameworks exist, some of the most widely recognized and utilized ones include the NIST Cybersecurity Framework, ISO 27001, and CIS Controls.

For instance, the NIST (National Institute of Standards and Technology) Cybersecurity Framework provides a flexible, risk-based approach that assists organizations in managing and reducing cybersecurity risk. It comprises five core functions: Identify, Protect, Detect, Respond, and Recover. These functions create a structured, iterative process that helps organizations assess their cybersecurity posture, identify vulnerabilities, and develop strategies to mitigate threats.

ISO 27001, on the other hand, is an internationally recognized standard that describes the requirements for establishing, implementing, maintaining, and continually enhancing an Information Security Management System (ISMS). It offers a systematic approach to managing information security risks, focusing on preserving information assets' confidentiality, integrity, and availability.

The CIS (Center for Internet Security) Controls provides a prioritized set of actions that help organizations mitigate the most common cyber threats. These controls are organized into three implementation groups based on an organization's size, complexity, and risk profile. They encompass various security measures, from basic hygiene to advanced threat mitigation.

Best practices in cybersecurity frameworks encompass a variety of measures that organizations should adopt to enhance their digital security.

Risk assessment and management are foundational best practices. Organizations must identify and evaluate potential threats, vulnerabilities, and the potential impact of cyber incidents. Understanding their risk profile allows them to allocate resources effectively and prioritize security efforts.

Access control is another critical aspect. Implementing stringent access control measures ensures that only the authorized personnel can access sensitive data and systems. The fundamental components are authentication mechanisms, strong password policies, and least privilege access principles.

Regular updates and patch management are essential. Keeping software, operating systems, and applications updated is crucial as many cyberattacks target known vulnerabilities that can be patched with updates. Timely patch management helps protect against these exploits.

Security awareness and training are key components of a robust cybersecurity strategy. Human error remains an important factor in cybersecurity incidents, and providing employees with cybersecurity training and fostering a culture of security awareness can minimize the risk of social engineering attacks, including phishing.

Incident response planning is crucial. Preparing for cyber incidents is as important as preventing them. Establishing an incident response plan that outlines how to detect, respond, as well as recover from security incidents is essential. Regular testing and updating of this plan ensure it remains effective.

Encryption and data protection are critical for safeguarding sensitive information. Protecting data at rest and in transit through encryption techniques, such as using secure protocols (e.g., HTTPS) and encrypting sensitive files and communications, helps ensure data remains confidential.

Network security, which involves firewalls, intrusion detection systems (IDS), and intrusion prevention systems (IPS), helps defend against network-based threats. Segmentation of networks and monitoring for unusual network activity are vital components.

Security patch management is another essential process. Establishing a robust process for managing security patches ensures that vulnerabilities are promptly addressed. This includes staying up to date with patches and testing them in a controlled environment to ensure they do not disrupt critical systems.

Third-party risk management is crucial. Organizations often rely on third-party vendors and service providers. Ensuring these partners maintain a strong cybersecurity posture is essential, as their vulnerabilities can become yours.

Continuous monitoring and threat detection are vital for proactive cybersecurity. Employing constant monitoring tools and threat detection systems can help organizations detect as well as respond to security incidents in real-time, enhancing their ability to mitigate threats before they escalate.

Despite the invaluable guidance offered by cybersecurity frameworks and best practices, their implementation can pose challenges. The dynamic nature of the threat landscape means that organizations must continuously adapt their cybersecurity strategies. Resource constraints can also be an issue, particularly for smaller organizations. However, they can prioritize essential security practices to maximize protection even with limited resources.

Achieving a balance between security and usability is an ongoing challenge. Overly strict security measures can hinder productivity, while too lax security can expose vulnerabilities. Striking the right balance requires thoroughly understanding an organization's specific needs and risk tolerance.

In conclusion, in the digital age, cybersecurity frameworks and best practices are indispensable tools for organizations and individuals seeking to navigate the dangerous waters of cyberspace. These frameworks offer structured approaches to assessing, managing, and mitigating cybersecurity risks, providing a roadmap for protecting digital assets and data. By adopting and adapting cybersecurity best practices, organizations can build resilient defenses against the ever-evolving threat landscape, safeguarding their digital realms and ensuring critical information's integrity, confidentiality, and availability.

CHAPTER II

The Role of Ethical Hacking

Introduction to ethical hacking

In an era marked by the ever-growing dependence on technology, the threat of cyberattacks looms larger than ever before. As organizations and individuals increasingly store their sensitive data and conduct critical operations online, the need for robust cybersecurity measures becomes paramount. This is where ethical hacking, also known as penetration testing or white-hat hacking, emerges as a crucial practice. Ethical hacking involves systematically and legally probing computer systems and networks to uncover vulnerabilities and weaknesses that malicious hackers could exploit. In this section, we will delve into the world of ethical hacking, exploring its significance, principles, and role in safeguarding the digital realm.

Ethical hacking is fundamentally distinct from its malicious counterpart. While malicious hackers seek to infiltrate systems for personal gain, cybercriminal activity, or espionage, ethical hackers are authorized individuals or teams hired to simulate cyberattacks ethically and controlled. They aim not to compromise security but to identify vulnerabilities and recommend strengthening a system's defenses. A proactive approach to security, ethical hacking enables organizations to fix vulnerabilities before malevolent actors can take use of them beforehand.

One of the fundamental principles underpinning ethical hacking is consent. Ethical hackers must obtain explicit permission from the system owner before commencing their assessments. This ensures that the testing is conducted within legal and ethical boundaries. Moreover, ethical hackers operate under a strict code of conduct that prohibits them from causing any harm to the target systems. Their activities focus solely on identifying and documenting vulnerabilities without any unauthorized access or data breaches.

The methodology employed by ethical hackers mirrors that of malicious hackers. They use diverse techniques, tools, and strategies to mimic potential threats. These may include vulnerability scanning, penetration testing, social engineering, and code analysis. The objective is to replicate actual attack scenarios in order to fully evaluate the security posture of a system. After that, ethical hackers gather all of their information into comprehensive reports and suggest remediation.

In a world where cyber threats are always evolving and becoming more sophisticated, ethical hacking is vital. Businesses that don't evaluate and strengthen their cybersecurity defenses run the risk of experiencing data breaches, monetary losses, and damage to their reputation. Being one step ahead of cybercriminals is possible for organizations through the proactive protection mechanism of ethical hacking. Organizations can effectively manage risks by patching vulnerabilities, improving security policies, and strategically allocating resources by detecting them before they can be exploited.

Furthermore, ethical hacking is not confined to the corporate world alone. Governments, military entities, and critical infrastructure providers also rely on ethical hackers to protect national security interests. As our society becomes more interconnected and reliant on digital infrastructure, the consequences of cyberattacks on critical systems become increasingly severe. Ethical hackers play a pivotal role in safeguarding these vital components of our modern lives.

In conclusion, ethical hacking is a critical discipline that serves as a proactive defense against the ever-present threat of cyberattacks. By systematically assessing and identifying vulnerabilities in computer systems and networks, ethical hackers empower organizations to strengthen their cybersecurity measures. With its foundation in consent, ethics, and a commitment to non-destructive testing, ethical hacking is a force for good in an increasingly digital world. It enables us to navigate the digital landscape with greater confidence, knowing that individuals and teams are dedicated to keeping our systems secure from malicious intrusions.

Ethics and legality in hacking

In the realm of hacking, ethics and legality are two closely intertwined but distinct aspects that profoundly shape the actions and consequences of individuals involved in this field. Hacking, broadly defined as gaining unauthorized access to computer systems or networks, carries a complex web of moral and legal considerations. This section explores the ethical and legal dimensions of hacking, shedding light on the various perspectives and challenges surrounding this multifaceted topic.

Ethics in hacking are a matter of profound significance. Hacking activities can vary widely, from benevolent actions aimed at identifying and fixing security vulnerabilities (ethical hacking or penetration testing) to malicious intrusions meant to steal data, disrupt systems, or engage in cyber espionage. Ethical hackers, also known as white-hat hackers, adhere to a strict code of conduct that centers on obtaining explicit permission before probing systems, causing no harm, and reporting their findings to improve cybersecurity. Their ethical stance emphasizes the greater good of securing digital infrastructure and protecting individuals' privacy. However, the line between ethical and unethical hacking is often blurry, and ethical considerations can differ among individuals and cultures.

The ethical complexity of hacking becomes even more pronounced when considering hacktivism, a form of hacking aimed at promoting political or social causes. While hacktivists may believe that their actions serve a just cause, they often engage in illegal activities, raising ethical questions about the means used to achieve their ends. Is breaking the law to expose governmental wrongdoing or promote a particular ideology ethically justifiable? These questions spark intense debate among scholars, activists, and policymakers, highlighting the nuanced nature of hacking ethics.

On the legal front, hacking activities are governed by a complex web of national and international laws. As per the Computer Fraud and Abuse Act (CFAA) of the US and comparable laws in other nations, illegal access to computer networks or systems is typically prohibited. Legal frameworks differ from jurisdiction to jurisdiction, making it challenging to determine the precise legal status of hacking actions globally. Furthermore, the rapid evolution of technology often outpaces the development of new legislation, leaving legal gaps and ambiguities.

One legal aspect that complicates the hacking landscape is the international nature of cybercrime. Cybercriminals can launch assaults from anywhere in the world, and since hacking has no geographical boundaries, it is challenging for law enforcement to find and prosecute offenders. Therefore, successful management of cyber threats depends on international cooperation and agreements like the Budapest Convention on Cybercrime.

In recent years, ethical hacking has become more widely acknowledged as a useful technique for detecting and reducing cybersecurity threats. Many organizations hire ethical hackers to conduct penetration tests and vulnerability assessments to bolster their defenses. In this context, laws may protect ethical hackers acting within the boundaries of their authorized testing agreements. However, the legal landscape remains dynamic, and ethical hackers must navigate the intricacies of both national and international laws to ensure their activities stay within legal bounds.

In conclusion, ethics and legality in hacking are intertwined aspects that shape the actions and consequences of individuals in this field. Ethical considerations vary, and ethical and unethical hacking boundaries can be hazy. While essential for maintaining order in cyberspace, legal frameworks are complex and sometimes inadequate. As technology evolves, the dialogue surrounding hacking ethics and legality will remain an ongoing and multifaceted conversation, shaping the future of cybersecurity and digital ethics.

Differentiating ethical hackers from malicious hackers

In the intricate hacking world, individuals' motivations and objectives can significantly vary, leading to a fundamental distinction between ethical hackers and malicious hackers. These two groups may share technical skills, but their intentions, actions, and impacts diverge dramatically. This section aims to elucidate the critical differences that separate ethical hackers from their malicious counterparts, highlighting the ethical and practical considerations that define their roles in the digital landscape.

Ethical hackers, often called white-hat hackers, are individuals or cybersecurity professionals who engage in hacking activities with the explicit authorization and consent of the target systems' owners. They operate within strict ethical boundaries and legal frameworks, adhering to a code of conduct that emphasizes the responsible and constructive use of their skills. Finding vulnerabilities and weaknesses in computer systems, networks, or applications is the main goal of ethical hackers. They employ various hacking techniques and tools to simulate potential threats realistically. Ethical hackers do not seek personal gain, harm, or unauthorized access; instead, they aim to improve cybersecurity by proactively identifying and addressing weaknesses. Their findings are meticulously documented and shared with the organization or individual that hired them, enabling the strengthening of security measures and the protection of sensitive data.

In stark contrast, malicious hackers, often termed black-hat hackers, engage in hacking activities for personal gain, harm, or unauthorized access to computer systems or networks. Their motivations may include financial theft, data breaches, cyber espionage, or even mere disruption of services. Malicious hackers operate outside the boundaries of legality and ethics, using their technical prowess to exploit vulnerabilities for personal benefit or to the detriment of others. Their actions can result in significant harm, including financial losses, data breaches, and reputational damage to individuals, organizations, or even nations. Malicious hackers are driven by self-interest and criminal intent, often concealing their identities and locations to evade law enforcement.

While the ethical distinctions between white-hat and black-hat hackers seem clear-cut, the digital landscape is not without its gray areas and ethical dilemmas. Some hackers, known as gray-hat hackers, operate in a morally ambiguous space. They may discover vulnerabilities without formal authorization and then attempt to inform the affected party, often in exchange for a bounty or reward. While their intentions may be relatively benign compared to malicious hackers, their actions may still skirt the boundaries of legality and ethics, raising questions about their motivations and methods.

Ethical hacking plays a crucial role in safeguarding the digital realm. Organizations, governments, and individuals increasingly rely on ethical hackers to assess their cybersecurity posture proactively. Data breaches, monetary losses, and reputational harm can be avoided thanks to ethical hackers' ability to spot vulnerabilities before malevolent hackers can take advantage of them. They are valuable allies in the ongoing battle to protect sensitive information and critical infrastructure.

In conclusion, ethical and malicious hackers represent two fundamentally different approaches to hacking, driven by contrasting motivations and ethical principles. Ethical hackers operate within legal boundaries, seeking to enhance cybersecurity and protect digital assets, while malicious hackers pursue personal gain or harm. The differentiation between these two groups underscores the critical importance of ethical hacking in fortifying our digital defenses and maintaining the integrity of the digital world. While ethical hacking serves as a proactive and responsible approach to cybersecurity, it also highlights the need for robust legal frameworks and international cooperation to address the ongoing challenges of malicious hackers.

The significance of penetration testing

In an era marked by an ever-expanding digital landscape, the importance of cybersecurity cannot be overstated. Large and small organizations store vast amounts of sensitive data online, making them attractive targets for cybercriminals. As a result, safeguarding digital assets and ensuring the resilience of IT infrastructure have become paramount concerns. In this context, penetration testing, often called pen testing, emerges as a crucial practice. This section delves into the significance of penetration testing, highlighting its role in identifying vulnerabilities, enhancing cybersecurity, and fortifying digital defenses.

At its core, penetration testing is a simulated cyberattack conducted by cybersecurity professionals to uncover security weaknesses in a system or network. This process involves systematically probing for vulnerabilities, exploiting them (with permission), and evaluating the system's response to the attack. Similar to malevolent hackers, penetration testers use a variety of tools, approaches, and tactics to accurately simulate potential risks. The primary differentiation is found in the ethical and regulated approach of penetration testing, which guarantees that the target system is not harmed.

Penetration testing offers a practical evaluation of an organization's cybersecurity posture, which is one of its main advantages. While automated vulnerability scanning tools can identify known weaknesses, penetration testing goes beyond the surface, identifying complex vulnerabilities that may not be apparent through automated scans. This comprehensive approach helps organizations understand the full spectrum of risks they face, enabling them to prioritize remediation efforts effectively.

Furthermore, penetration testing allows organizations to address vulnerabilities proactively before malicious actors can exploit them. In today's threat landscape, cyberattacks constantly evolve, and attackers continually seek new avenues to breach defenses. Regular penetration testing helps organizations avoid these growing threats by identifying and mitigating vulnerabilities before they can be leveraged for malicious purposes. By taking a proactive approach, the likelihood of data breaches, monetary losses, and reputational harm can be considerably decreased.

Penetration testing also plays a crucial role in compliance and regulatory requirements. Many industries and regions have established cybersecurity standards and regulations that organizations must adhere to. Penetration testing is often required to comply with these standards, helping organizations demonstrate their commitment to security and risk management. Additionally, it provides evidence of due diligence in the event of an audit or data breach investigation.

Another significant aspect of penetration testing is its ability to assess an organization's incident response capabilities. The security team must detect and respond to the simulated attack during a penetration test. This process helps organizations evaluate the effectiveness of their security monitoring and incident response procedures. Identifying weaknesses in incident response allows organizations to refine their processes and better prepare for real-world cyber incidents.

In conclusion, penetration testing is critical to a comprehensive cybersecurity strategy. Its ability to identify vulnerabilities, provide real-world assessments, and enhance an organization's security posture makes it an indispensable tool in the fight against cyber threats. As the digital landscape continues to evolve, penetration testing remains essential for organizations seeking to protect sensitive data, maintain regulatory compliance, and stay one step ahead of cybercriminals. Organizations can proactively strengthen their defenses and lower the likelihood of becoming victims of cyberattacks in an increasingly interconnected world by periodically investing in penetration testing.

CHAPTER III

Cyber Threat Landscape

An overview of current cyber threats

In today's interconnected world, the digital landscape is a realm of innovation and opportunity and a battlefield where a constant struggle for control and dominance unfolds. This battle involves sophisticated, evolving, and pervasive cyber threats that threaten the security and integrity of digital systems, networks, and data. In this section, we provide an in-depth overview of current cyber threats, exploring the diverse range of risks organizations and individuals face in the digital age. From ransomware attacks to nation-state cyber espionage, understanding these threats is crucial for devising effective cybersecurity strategies and fortifying our defenses in this evolving digital battlefield.

Ransomware attacks have surged to the forefront of cyber threats in recent years. In these malicious efforts, data belonging to an organization is encrypted, and a ransom is demanded in return for the decryption key. Since ransomware may destroy companies, healthcare facilities, and even entire municipalities, it is very destructive. Attackers' strategies have changed over time, using more complex techniques, frequently focusing on critical infrastructure and using double-extortion tactics to put more pressure on victims.

Phishing and social engineering attacks are still a constant concern because they use psychological manipulation to deceive people, get access to systems without authorization, or steal private data. Cybercriminals employ convincing email, phone, or social media schemes to trick users into revealing passwords, financial data, or other confidential information. Individuals and organizations must remain vigilant as phishing attacks become more convincing and targeted.

Advanced Persistent Threats (APTs) represent a category of cyber threats often associated with nation-state actors. APTs are characterized by their long-term, highly targeted campaigns to compromise specific organizations, government agencies, or industries. These actors pursue diverse objectives, including espionage, intellectual property theft, and even potential disruption of critical infrastructure. APTs leverage advanced techniques to remain hidden within networks for extended periods, challenging detection and mitigation.

Zero-day vulnerabilities are software flaws unknown to the vendor and, therefore, unpatched. Cybercriminals and state-sponsored actors exploit these vulnerabilities to gain unauthorized access or launch attacks before developers can release security patches. The discovery and exploitation of zero-days pose significant risks, as they allow attackers to bypass conventional security measures.

Insider threats remain a significant concern, with both malicious insiders and unwitting employees posing risks to organizations. Malicious insiders may intentionally compromise data or systems, while negligent employees may inadvertently expose sensitive information through careless actions. Organizations must implement robust security measures, monitoring, and training to mitigate these threats.

The Internet of Things (IoT) devices proliferation has expanded the attack surface for cybercriminals. Many IoT devices lack robust security measures, making them vulnerable to exploitation. Cybercriminals can compromise these devices to launch attacks or gain unauthorized network access. Protecting IoT ecosystems requires improved device security and network segmentation.

Supply chain attacks involve infiltrating an organization's network through vulnerabilities in its suppliers or partners. Attackers recognize that organizations often overlook the security of their supply chains. Recent high-profile supply chain attacks have exposed the risks associated with these tactics, highlighting the need for enhanced supplier security assessments.

Cloud security has become a prominent concern as organizations increasingly migrate to cloud environments. Misconfigurations, inadequate access controls, and unpatched vulnerabilities in cloud services can expose sensitive data to unauthorized access. Securing cloud environments requires a shared responsibility model, with organizations and cloud providers collaborating to ensure robust protection.

State-sponsored cyber operations are a global concern, with nation-states engaging in cyber espionage, disinformation campaigns, and potentially disruptive activities. These operations can target critical infrastructure, government institutions, and commercial entities. The blurred lines between cybercrime and state-sponsored activities complicate attribution and response efforts.

An often underestimated challenge in cybersecurity is the shortage of skilled professionals. The demand for cybersecurity experts far outpaces the supply, creating a skills gap that organizations struggle to fill. Addressing this gap requires investments in education, training, and cultivating diverse talent.

Cyber threats are dynamic and ever-evolving, reflecting the rapid advancement of technology and the ingenuity of malicious actors. These threats span a broad spectrum, from financially motivated cybercriminals to nation-state actors pursuing geopolitical objectives. Understanding the current cyber threat landscape is essential for individuals, organizations, and governments alike. It informs the development of robust cybersecurity strategies, the implementation of effective defenses, and the adaptation to emerging threats. In this digital age, vigilance, preparedness, and collaboration are key in the ongoing battle to safeguard our digital assets and protect our interconnected world from the relentless tide of cyber threats.

Types of cyberattacks (e.g., malware, phishing, DDoS)

In the vast and interconnected landscape of the digital world, cyberattacks have become an ever-present and constantly evolving menace. These attacks, often carried out by malicious actors with diverse motivations, target individuals, organizations, and even nations, posing substantial risks to data security, privacy, and digital infrastructure. In this section, we delve into the various types of cyberattacks, shedding light on the mechanics, objectives, and consequences of these digital assaults. From the insidious spread of malware to the deceptive art of phishing and the disruptive power of Distributed Denial of Service (DDoS) attacks, understanding these threats is essential for fortifying our defenses in the digital age.

Malicious software, called malware for short, is a broad category of cyberattacks encompassing viruses, worms, Trojans, spyware, and ransomware, among others. Malware primarily aims to infiltrate, disrupt, or gain unauthorized access to computer systems and networks. Viruses and worms spread through infected files or emails, while Trojans masquerade as legitimate software to deceive users. Spyware covertly collects sensitive information, and ransomware encrypts files and demands a ransom for decryption keys. The consequences of malware attacks range from data theft to system compromise, with ransomware attacks often leading to financial extortion.

Phishing attacks use social engineering and deceit to fool people into disclosing personal information, financial information, or login credentials. These attacks often involve fraudulent emails or websites that impersonate trusted entities, like banks, social media platforms, or government agencies. Cybercriminals use enticing messages or threats to manipulate users into taking action, such as clicking malicious links or downloading attachments. Phishing attacks can lead to identity theft, financial fraud, and data breaches, making them a prevalent and insidious threat.

DDoS (Distributed Denial of Service) attacks are made to overwhelm a target's network or online services by flooding them with massive traffic, rendering them inaccessible to legitimate users. Attackers typically use networks of compromised devices, known as botnets, to orchestrate these assaults. DDoS attacks disrupt online operations, causing downtime, financial losses, and reputational damage. These attacks can have far-reaching consequences, affecting businesses, government agencies, and critical infrastructure.

Ransomware attacks have gained notoriety for their ability to encrypt an organization's data and demand a ransom in exchange for the decryption key. These attacks can destroy businesses and institutions, resulting in financial losses and operational disruptions. Ransomware actors have evolved their tactics, employing double-extortion techniques, where stolen data is threatened with public exposure in addition to encryption. Recent high-profile ransomware attacks have underscored the urgency of robust defenses and incident response strategies.

Individuals who work for an organization and abuse their access to compromise systems or data, whether on purpose or accidentally, are the source of insider threats. Malicious insiders may have motives like financial gain or revenge, while negligent employees may inadvertently expose sensitive information through careless actions. Mitigating insider threats requires a combination of technical controls, employee training, and monitoring to detect unusual behavior.

Man-in-the-Middle (MitM) attacks take place when a third party, usually without the victim's knowledge, intercepts or modifies communication between two parties. These attacks target various communication channels, including Wi-Fi networks, email, and web traffic. Cybercriminals use MitM attacks to eavesdrop on sensitive data, inject malicious content, or impersonate one of the parties involved. Securing communication channels with encryption and robust authentication measures can mitigate the risks of MitM attacks.

SQL injection attacks target web applications by exploiting vulnerabilities in their databases. Attackers inject malicious SQL queries into input fields, tricking the application into executing unintended database commands. This can result in unauthorized access, data theft, or even a compromise of the entire application. Proper input validation and parameterized queries are essential defenses against SQL injection.

Zero-day exploits target vulnerabilities in software that are unknown to the vendor or unpatched. Cybercriminals discover and exploit these vulnerabilities before developers release security patches, making them especially dangerous. Organizations must employ proactive security measures, including vulnerability scanning and threat intelligence, to detect and defend against zero-day exploits.

Supply chain attacks involve infiltrating an organization's network through vulnerabilities in its suppliers or partners. Attackers recognize that organizations often overlook the security of their supply chains. Recent high- profile supply chain attacks have exposed the risks associated with these tactics, highlighting the need for enhanced supplier security assessments.

State-sponsored cyber operations involve nations using cyberattacks for espionage, disinformation, or potentially disruptive activities. These operations can target critical infrastructure, government institutions, and commercial entities. Attributing state-sponsored attacks can be complex, blurring the lines between cybercrime and geopolitical maneuvering.

In conclusion, the digital age has ushered in a complex and diverse landscape of cyber threats, each with its mechanics, objectives, and consequences. These threats span from the covert infiltration of malware to the deceptive tactics of phishing, the disruptive power of DDoS attacks, and the excessive nature of ransomware. Understanding these cyber threats is essential for individuals, organizations, and governments to fortify their defenses, respond effectively to incidents, and safeguard the integrity and security of digital systems, data, and infrastructure. In the ongoing battle against cyber adversaries, vigilance, resilience, and a commitment to cybersecurity are paramount in navigating the digital frontier.

Real-world examples of major cyber incidents

In the ever-evolving landscape of the digital age, major cyber incidents have become a stark reality, affecting individuals, organizations, and nations on a global scale. These incidents span a broad spectrum, from data breaches that expose sensitive information to disruptive ransomware attacks that paralyze critical infrastructure.

This section delves into real-world examples of major cyber incidents, exploring the causes, impacts, and lessons learned from these digital disasters. From the infamous Equifax breach to the destructive NotPetya malware outbreak and the SolarWinds supply chain attack, these incidents offer valuable insights into the evolving nature of cyber threats and the imperative of robust cybersecurity practices.

The Equifax data breach of 2017 ranks among the most notorious cyber incidents in recent history. This breach exposed sensitive personal information of approximately 143 million Americans, including Social Security numbers, birthdates, and financial records. The breach happened because of the vulnerability in Equifax's website software, which the company failed to patch promptly. The fallout from the breach was significant, leading to congressional hearings, executive resignations, and a loss of trust among consumers. The incident underscored the critical importance of timely patching, vulnerability management, and robust security measures to protect sensitive data.

NotPetya, a strain of ransomware that emerged in 2017, marked a significant shift in cyber threats. Initially disguised as a ransomware attack, it quickly became evident that the malware had a destructive intent. NotPetya spread rapidly through vulnerable systems, encrypting files and rendering them irrecoverable. Victims included major multinational corporations and critical infrastructure providers. The attack disrupted operations, causing financial losses estimated in the billions. NotPetya demonstrated that ransomware attacks could have far-reaching consequences beyond financial extortion, highlighting the need for robust incident response and recovery plans.

The SolarWinds supply chain attack, discovered in late 2020, was a sophisticated and highly impactful cyber incident. It involved the compromise of SolarWinds' software update mechanism, which allowed attackers to distribute a backdoored version of the company's Orion software to thousands of organizations, like government agencies and Fortune 500 companies. This covert intrusion enabled the attackers to gain unauthorized access to sensitive networks and conduct espionage. The incident exposed the vulnerabilities inherent in supply chain security and the challenges of detecting and mitigating advanced threats.

When the WannaCry ransomware attacked hundreds of thousands of computers across more than 150 countries in 2017, it garnered attention. Exploiting a vulnerability in Microsoft Windows, the malware encrypted files and demanded a ransom for decryption. Hospitals, government agencies, and businesses were among the victims. The incident highlighted the urgency of patch management and the risks associated with using outdated and unsupported software. It also emphasized the need for international cooperation to combat cyber threats.

In May 2021, the Colonial Pipeline, which supplies a significant portion of the East Coast's fuel, fell victim to a ransomware attack attributed to the DarkSide hacking group. The attack forced the pipeline operator to shut down its operations, causing fuel shortages and price spikes in several states. The incident underscored the vulnerability of critical infrastructure to cyberattacks and the potential real-world consequences of ransomware attacks. It also prompted discussions about the need for enhanced cybersecurity measures in critical sectors.

Stuxnet, discovered in 2010, was a groundbreaking cyber weapon attributed to nation-state actors. It targeted supervisory control and data acquisition, or SCADA systems used in Iran's nuclear program. Stuxnet demonstrated the potential of cyberattacks to disrupt physical infrastructure, such as centrifuges used in uranium enrichment. This incident raised concerns about the militarization of cyberspace and the blurred lines between cyber espionage and cyber warfare.

The Target data breach of 2013 exposed credit and debit card data of over 40 million customers. Attackers accessed Target's network through a third-party HVAC contractor and exploited the company's payment processing systems vulnerabilities. The breach had far-reaching consequences, including financial losses and damaging Target's reputation. It emphasized the need for organizations to secure third-party access and implement robust intrusion detection and response systems.

The Sony Pictures hack in 2014 was notable for its impact on both a major corporation and international relations. Attackers, reportedly linked to North Korea, breached Sony Pictures' network, stealing sensitive corporate data and releasing it publicly. The incident was believed to be retaliation for releasing a controversial film. It highlighted the use of cyberattacks for political and geopolitical purposes, raising concerns about cyber threats in the context of freedom of expression and international diplomacy.

The Heartbleed vulnerability, disclosed in 2014, exposed a critical flaw in the OpenSSL cryptographic library—a core component of internet security infrastructure. The bug allowed attackers to steal sensitive data from vulnerable servers, including passwords and encryption keys. Heartbleed affected a wide range of online services, making it a significant cybersecurity incident. It emphasized the importance of rigorous code review and the need for timely patching in open-source software.

In 2014, JPMorgan Chase, one of the largest banks in the United States, suffered a significant data breach. Attackers accessed the bank's network, compromising the data of over 76 million households as well as 7 million small businesses. The breach highlighted the risks faced by financial institutions and the need for robust cybersecurity measures in the banking sector.

In conclusion, real-world examples of major cyber incidents serve as stark reminders of cyber threats' evolving nature and far-reaching consequences. From data breaches that undermine trust to destructive ransomware attacks that disrupt critical infrastructure, these incidents underscore the imperative of proactive cybersecurity practices, timely patch management, supply chain security, and international cooperation. As cyber threats continue to evolve, vigilance, resilience, and a commitment to cybersecurity remain paramount in defending against digital disasters and securing the interconnected world in which we live.

The financial and reputational impact of cyberattacks

In today's interconnected digital world, cyberattack threats loom larger than ever. Cybercriminals, equipped with increasingly sophisticated tools and techniques, target organizations across industries and individuals alike. These cyberattacks' financial and reputational consequences are substantial, often causing significant damage that extends far beyond the initial breach. This section explores the multifaceted impact of cyberattacks, delving into the financial losses and reputational harm that organizations and individuals can suffer as a result.

The financial repercussions of a cyberattack can be staggering. The immediate costs include expenses related to incident response, such as hiring cybersecurity experts to investigate the breach, legal fees, and the costs associated with notifying affected parties and regulatory authorities. Organizations may also need to invest in system repairs and upgrades to address vulnerabilities and prevent future breaches.

Data breaches, one of the most common forms of cyberattacks, can lead to substantial financial losses. Cybercriminals often steal sensitive information, such as customer data, intellectual property, or financial records, which can have severe financial implications. Organizations may face fines and penalties for failing to protect this data adequately, especially if they are subject to data protection regulations including General Data Protection Regulation (GDPR) of European Union or the California Consumer Privacy Act (CCPA). Additionally, the costs associated with providing identity theft protection services to affected individuals can be substantial.

The loss of business continuity is another financial consequence of cyberattacks. When systems are compromised or taken offline during an attack, organizations suffer downtime, which can result in lost revenue and productivity. In some cases, cyberattacks can destroy or steal critical data, causing irreparable harm to an organization's operations and bottom line.

A cyberattack can generate reputational damage that can last longer than the immediate monetary losses. Trust is a cornerstone of any successful business or organization, and a cyberattack can erode that trust rapidly. When customers, clients, or partners learn that their personal or sensitive information has been compromised, they often lose confidence in the affected organization's ability to protect their data.

Reputation damage can result in a loss of customers and revenue. Individuals and businesses may sever their ties with an organization following a cyberattack, opting for competitors they perceive as more secure. Moreover, negative media coverage and public scrutiny can exacerbate the reputational harm, tarnishing an organization's brand for years to come.

Beyond customer trust, the trust of shareholders, investors, and partners can also be eroded. A high-profile cyberattack can lead to a drop in stock prices, and investors may lose confidence in an organization's leadership and cybersecurity measures. Partnerships and collaborations can be strained or terminated as organizations seek to protect their own reputations by disassociating from the affected party.

Recovering from reputational damage is a long and arduous process. Organizations must invest in public relations efforts, marketing campaigns, and ongoing transparency to rebuild stakeholder trust. Even then, the memory of a cyberattack can linger, and some damage may be irreparable.

In conclusion, cyberattacks' financial and reputational impact is profound and far-reaching. The financial costs include immediate incident response expenses, fines, data recovery, and lost revenue due to downtime. On the other hand, reputational damage can cause investors, partners, and consumers to lose trust in a company, which can have a long-term negative impact on its financial line and brand. One cannot stress the value of strong cybersecurity safeguards and incident response plans in the ever-evolving digital ecosystem. In an interconnected world, organizations and individuals alike need to focus on cybersecurity to lessen the severe financial and reputational effects of cyberattacks.

CHAPTER IV

Cybersecurity Tools and Technologies

Overview of essential cybersecurity tools

The battle between defenders and malicious actors is ongoing in the rapidly evolving landscape of cybersecurity. Organizations and individuals must employ a robust arsenal of tools and technologies to protect sensitive data, digital assets, and critical infrastructure from the relentless tide of cyber threats. This section provides an overview of essential cybersecurity tools that form the foundation of a comprehensive cybersecurity strategy. Protecting the digital world from a variety of cyberthreats requires the use of technologies such as intrusion detection systems, firewalls, antivirus software, and encryption tools.

Firewalls are one of the foundational elements of cybersecurity, serving as the gatekeepers that control network traffic. These hardware or software-based solutions establish a barrier between an organization's internal network and external, potentially untrusted sources, allowing only authorized traffic to pass through. Firewalls are essential for blocking unauthorized access attempts, preventing malware from infiltrating the network, and ensuring that only legitimate data transmissions occur.

Antivirus software is crucial in identifying and mitigating malware threats. These tools scan files, applications, and network traffic for known malware signatures and behavior patterns. When a threat is detected, antivirus software can quarantine or remove the malicious code, preventing it from causing harm. While antivirus software is effective against known threats, it's important to complement it with other security measures since it may not always detect zero-day vulnerabilities or sophisticated malware.

Intrusion Detection Systems (or IDS) and Intrusion Prevention Systems (or IPS) are essential for proactive threat defense. IDS monitors network traffic for suspicious activity, such as unusual traffic patterns or known attack signatures, and generates alerts when potential threats are detected. On the other hand, IPS detects threats and takes automated action to block or mitigate them in real-time. These tools are instrumental in identifying and responding to cyber threats swiftly.

Virtual Private Networks (VPNs) are indispensable for securing communication channels, particularly in remote work environments. VPNs encrypt data traffic between a user's device and a remote server, ensuring that sensitive information remains confidential even when transmitted over untrusted networks like the internet. They are widely used to protect data privacy and maintain the security of remote access to corporate networks.

Encryption is a fundamental cybersecurity technique that protects data at rest (when stored) and in transit (when transmitted). Complex algorithms are used by encryption technologies to jumble data, rendering it unintelligible without the matching decryption key. This safeguards sensitive information from unauthorized access, even if it falls into the wrong hands. End-to-end encryption for messaging apps and full-disk encryption for devices are common applications of encryption tools.

SIEM, or the Security Information and Event Management solutions provide centralized monitoring and analysis of security events and data across an organization's network. SIEM tools collect and correlate data from various sources, such as logs, sensors, and security devices, to identify patterns indicative of security incidents. They play a critical role in incident detection, investigation, and response.

Penetration testing tools, often used by ethical hackers, allow organizations to assess their network and application vulnerabilities proactively. These tools simulate cyberattacks to identify weaknesses in security defenses. By conducting penetration tests, organizations can uncover vulnerabilities before malicious actors exploit them, enabling timely remediation and risk reduction.

Multi-Factor Authentication, or MFA, fortifies user authentication procedures with an additional layer of protection. Instead of relying solely on passwords, MFA requires users to provide multiple verification forms, such as a password, a fingerprint, or a one-time code sent to a mobile device. This significantly enhances access controls and mitigates the risks associated with password-based attacks.

Patch management tools are essential for maintaining the security of software and systems. These tools automate identifying, downloading, and applying security patches and updates. Keeping software up to date is crucial for addressing known vulnerabilities and minimizing the risk of exploitation by cybercriminals.

Network monitoring tools provide real-time visibility into an organization's network, allowing for continuous surveillance of traffic and system performance. These tools help identify anomalies, unauthorized access, and potential security incidents. They are invaluable for maintaining network integrity and early threat detection.

In conclusion, essential cybersecurity tools constitute a robust defense against cyber threats in our digital age. From firewalls that guard network perimeters to antivirus software that detects and removes malware, and from encryption tools that protect data privacy to penetration testing tools that assess vulnerabilities, these technologies work together to create layers of protection. In an ever-evolving threat landscape, organizations and individuals must leverage these tools effectively to safeguard their digital assets, data, and systems from the persistent and evolving challenges posed by cyber threats.

Antivirus software and firewalls

In the ever-evolving cybersecurity landscape, two foundational components are critical defenses against various threats: antivirus software and firewalls. These tools play distinct but complementary roles in safeguarding computer systems and networks from malicious actors. This section explores the significance of antivirus software and firewalls in cybersecurity, highlighting their functions, benefits, and vital role in maintaining digital security.

Antivirus software, often called antivirus or anti-malware software, is a fundamental cybersecurity tool designed to detect, avoid, and remove malicious software, commonly known as malware. Malware encompasses a broad category of threats, including viruses, worms, Trojans, ransomware, spyware, and adware, each with its own modus operandi and potential for harm.

The primary usage of antivirus software is to scan files, programs, and the entire system for known patterns or signatures of malware. When it identifies a match, it quarantines or removes the malicious code to prevent it from causing harm. Modern antivirus solutions employ heuristic analysis and behavior-based detection methods, allowing them to detect and mitigate previously unseen or zero-day threats.

Antivirus software also plays a crucial role in real-time protection. It monitors incoming and outgoing network traffic, email attachments, and file downloads to intercept and neutralize threats before they can infiltrate a system or network. By regularly updating its virus signature database and maintaining a comprehensive threat intelligence network, antivirus software remains equipped to combat the ever-evolving threat landscape.

Another essential cybersecurity tool is a firewall, which acts as a roadblock between an internal network that is trustworthy and untrusted external networks like the internet. As gatekeepers, firewalls examine all incoming and outgoing network traffic in accordance with pre-established rules and policies. Their primary objective is to permit legitimate traffic while blocking or filtering unauthorized or potentially harmful data packets.

Firewalls come in two main types: hardware firewalls and software firewalls. Hardware firewalls are typically deployed at the network perimeter, such as at the entry point of an organization's network. They are responsible for filtering traffic entering and leaving the entire network. On the other hand, software firewalls are installed on individual devices, such as computers or smartphones, and monitor traffic specific to that device.

To analyze network traffic, firewalls utilize various filtering techniques, including packet filtering, stateful inspection, and deep packet inspection (DPI). These techniques enable firewalls to determine whether data packets meet the defined security criteria and should be allowed to pass or be blocked.

One of the significant advantages of firewalls is their ability to establish security zones or segmented network architectures. Organizations can enhance security by isolating critical assets from less secure areas by dividing the network into distinct zones with varying levels of trust. Firewalls play a pivotal role in enforcing these segmentation policies, preventing unauthorized access and lateral movement by cyber attackers.

Antivirus software and firewalls work hand in hand to provide comprehensive cybersecurity protection. While antivirus software focuses on identifying and neutralizing malicious code, firewalls safeguard network traffic and control resource access. Together, they create layers of defense that significantly reduce the attack surface and mitigate a wide range of threats.

Antivirus software excels at identifying and eradicating malware that may have evaded network defenses. Conversely, firewalls prevent unauthorized access to the network and protect against threats that attempt to exploit vulnerabilities in network services. This complementary approach ensures that even if a malicious file or program reaches a device, it is less likely to communicate with external malicious servers or spread laterally across the network.

In conclusion, antivirus software and firewalls are integral components of modern cybersecurity. Antivirus software identifies and neutralizes malware, while firewalls control network traffic and access. Together, they form a robust defense against diverse cyber threats, helping individuals and organizations protect their digital assets, maintain data integrity, and ensure the confidentiality of sensitive information. As the cybersecurity landscape continues to evolve, antivirus software and firewalls remain indispensable tools in the ongoing battle against cyber threats.

Intrusion Detection and Prevention Systems (IDPS)

In the ever-evolving realm of cybersecurity, Intrusion Detection and Prevention Systems (IDPS) stand as formidable gatekeepers, diligently monitoring network traffic and actively defending against intrusions and cyberattacks. IDPS represents a critical component of an organization's security infrastructure, offering the ability to detect and respond to suspicious and malicious activities in real-time. In this section, we delve into the multifaceted world of IDPS, exploring its key functions, deployment strategies, challenges, and its pivotal role in enhancing cybersecurity posture.

IDPS, as the name suggests, serves a dual purpose: intrusion detection and intrusion prevention. These systems are designed to identify and respond to activities that deviate from normal, authorized patterns within a network. To accomplish this, IDPS employs various techniques, including signature-based detection, anomaly-based detection, and behavioral analysis.

Signature-based detection involves comparing network traffic and data packets to a known attack signatures or patterns database. When a match is found, indicating a known threat or attack, the IDPS generates an alert or takes predefined actions to thwart the intrusion. Anomaly-based detection focuses on identifying deviations from established baselines of network behavior. IDPS continuously monitors network traffic, building a profile of normal activities. When it detects behavior that falls outside these established norms, it raises an alarm, suspecting a potential intrusion or security incident. On the other hand, behavioral analysis analyzes the behavior of applications and users to identify unusual or suspicious actions that may indicate an intrusion. By examining how applications interact with each other and how users typically access resources, behavioral analysis helps detect novel threats and zero-day attacks.

IDPS can be deployed in various ways, depending on an organization's needs and network architecture. Network-based IDPS (NIDPS) is positioned at strategic points within a network, typically at network boundaries or chokepoints, to monitor all traffic passing through those points. It is well-suited for detecting threats targeting network infrastructure. On the other hand, host-based

IDPS (HIDPS) is installed on individual hosts or endpoints, such as servers and workstations. It monitors activities on the host itself, effectively identifying attacks that may originate from within the network. Cloud-based IDPS (CIDPS) operates in the cloud infrastructure to monitor traffic and activities across cloud services and resources, which is particularly valuable for securing cloud-hosted applications and data. Some organizations opt for a combination of NIDPS, HIDPS, and CIDPS to create a comprehensive defense-in-depth strategy, allowing for the detection of threats at multiple levels of the network.

While IDPS is a powerful cybersecurity tool, its implementation has challenges and considerations. It can generate false positives (mistakenly identifying benign activities as threats) and false negatives (failing to detect actual threats), necessitating fine-tuning to reduce these instances and avoid alert fatigue. Encrypted traffic can pose challenges for IDPS, as it can't inspect the content of encrypted packets. Advanced IDPS solutions include SSL/TLS decryption capabilities to address this issue. Additionally, IDPS must balance sensitivity to detect threats and minimize false alarms, requiring continuous tuning and adjustment to adapt to changing network conditions and threats. Proper sizing and resource allocation are crucial to avoid performance bottlenecks, as IDPS can be resource-intensive and may introduce latency into high-speed networks.

In conclusion, Intrusion Detection and Prevention Systems (IDPS) are the vigilant guardians of network security, tirelessly monitoring network traffic, identifying threats, and actively defending against intrusions. Their role in early threat detection, zero-day threat mitigation, automated response, and incident investigation is invaluable in the ever-evolving landscape of cybersecurity. IDPS continues to be a vital part of an all-encompassing cybersecurity strategy, protecting networks from malevolent actors and guaranteeing the integrity and security of digital assets as enterprises confront more complex and persistent cyberthreats.

Security Information and Event Management (SIEM) systems

In the complex and dynamic landscape of cybersecurity, organizations are constantly challenged by the need to detect and respond to many security threats and incidents. Systems like Security Information and Event Management, also known as SIEM have become essential resources because they provide a centralized environment for gathering, examining, and comparing security data from many sources. SIEM systems enhance an organization's cybersecurity posture by providing real-time insights, facilitating incident response, and ensuring compliance with regulatory requirements. In this section, we explore the multifaceted world of SIEM systems, delving into their key functions, components, deployment strategies, challenges, and their crucial role in modern cybersecurity.

At its core, a SIEM system is a centralized platform designed to ingest, process, and analyze vast volumes of security-related data generated by an organization's IT infrastructure and security tools. This data includes logs and events from various sources, such as network devices, servers, endpoints, applications, and security appliances. SIEM systems serve as the nerve center for an organization's cybersecurity operations, providing a unified view of its security posture.

SIEM systems perform several key functions. Firstly, they collect and aggregate logs and events from various sources, including firewalls, intrusion detection systems, antivirus software, and more. This data is normalized to ensure consistency and ease of analysis. Secondly, SIEM systems engage in event correlation, which involves analyzing the collected data to identify patterns and anomalies that may indicate security threats or incidents. Correlation rules and algorithms are applied to detect potentially malicious activities. When SIEM detects suspicious or malicious activities, it generates alerts and notifications, typically categorized by severity, enabling security teams to prioritize their response efforts. Additionally, SIEM systems facilitate incident response by providing real-time information about security incidents. Security teams can use the data and alerts provided by the SIEM to investigate incidents, take action, and mitigate potential damage. Lastly, SIEM often includes reporting capabilities that help organizations meet regulatory compliance requirements. They can generate predefined reports and allow for custom reporting to demonstrate adherence to security policies and regulations.

SIEM systems consist of several vital components. Data collectors gather log and event data from various sources, normalize it, and transmit it to the central SIEM platform for analysis. The event database stores the collected data, making it available for correlation, analysis, and reporting. The correlation engine applies predefined correlation rules and algorithms to the data to identify security incidents and patterns of concern. The alerting and notification system generates alerts and notifications based on correlation results and sends them to security personnel for further action. Finally, SIEM systems often provide user-friendly dashboards for real-time monitoring and reporting capabilities to generate historical reports on security events and incidents.

Organizations can deploy SIEM systems in various ways, depending on their specific needs and infrastructure. On-premises SIEM involves installing and managing the SIEM solution within the organization's own data center. This provides full control over the system but requires significant hardware and personnel resources for maintenance. Cloud-based SIEM solutions are hosted in the cloud and offered as a service, reducing the burden of infrastructure management and can be cost-effective for organizations with limited resources. Some organizations opt for a hybrid approach, combining on-premises and cloud-based SIEM components to address specific requirements or compliance needs.

While SIEM systems offer potent capabilities for enhancing cybersecurity, their implementation presents challenges and considerations. Organizations generate immense volumes of data daily, leading to high-security alerts. Filtering out false positives and identifying true threats can be challenging. SIEM systems can be complex to implement and maintain, especially in large organizations. Scalability is crucial to ensure that the SIEM can handle growing data volumes. Effective use of SIEM requires skilled personnel who can interpret alerts, investigate incidents, and fine-tune the system for optimal performance. Integration with existing security tools and infrastructure is essential for maximizing effectiveness. Meeting compliance requirements, like GDPR or HIPAA, can be complex and requires careful configuration and reporting within the SIEM.

In today's cybersecurity landscape, SIEM systems are pivotal in helping organizations detect and respond to security threats efficiently. They provide real-time visibility into network activity, facilitate rapid incident response, and aid in compliance efforts. SIEM systems enable organizations to stay one step ahead of cyber adversaries, making informed decisions to protect critical assets and data. As cyber threats evolve in sophistication and frequency, SIEM systems remain essential for organizations committed to safeguarding their digital resources and maintaining a robust cybersecurity posture.

Encryption and data protection

In the ever-expanding digital landscape, data has become the lifeblood of organizations and individuals alike. Data security and confidentiality are paramount with the proliferation of digital transactions, communications, and storage. Encryption is a fundamental pillar of cybersecurity, offering a robust means to protect data from unauthorized access and interception. This section explores the critical role of encryption in data protection, delving into its core principles, methods, challenges, and broader implications for the evolving cybersecurity world.

Encryption is converting plaintext, which is human-readable data, into ciphertext, an unreadable format without the appropriate decryption key. It safeguards against unauthorized access, ensuring that even if an attacker acquires access to the encrypted data, they cannot decrypt it without the encryption key. The fundamental principle behind encryption lies in using mathematical algorithms to transform data into a format that is unintelligible to anyone without the proper decryption credentials.

At its core, encryption consists of several vital components. Encryption algorithms are mathematical functions that determine how data is transformed into ciphertext. Modern encryption relies on robust and complex algorithms that are difficult to reverse engineer. Encryption keys are the secret codes or credentials used to encrypt and decrypt data. There are two primary types: symmetric encryption, which employs a single key for the encryption and decryption, and asymmetric encryption, which uses a pair of keys—a public key for encryption and a private key for decryption. Cryptographic protocols are sets of rules and standards that dictate how encryption should be applied in various contexts, such as secure communications (e.g., SSL/TLS for web traffic) and data storage (e.g., BitLocker for disk encryption).

Symmetric and the asymmetric encryption are two types of encryption techniques that use a pair of keys—a public key that is used for encryption and a private key for decryption—instead of a single key for both operations. Additionally, hash functions generate fixed-length strings of characters (hashes) from data and are used to verify data integrity and ensure it hasn't been tampered with.

Encryption is pivotal in modern cybersecurity for several reasons. Firstly, it ensures the confidentiality of sensitive data, protecting it from eavesdropping and unauthorized access. Secondly, encryption helps maintain data integrity by detecting any alterations or tampering attempts. It also plays a role in authentication protocols, confirming the identity of parties involved in data exchange. Encryption is essential for securing communication channels, such as email, messaging, and web traffic, protecting sensitive information during transit. Furthermore, it safeguards data at rest, whether on physical devices or in cloud storage, ensuring that even if storage media are compromised, the data remains unreadable without the encryption key.

Despite its critical role, encryption faces challenges in the cybersecurity landscape. Secure key management is essential to prevent unauthorized access, as the loss of encryption keys can make data permanently inaccessible. Encryption can introduce processing overhead, impacting the performance of systems, particularly in high-speed environments. The debate over encryption backdoors, which would allow authorized access to encrypted data, raises complex legal, ethical, and security concerns. Additionally, quantum computing could break existing encryption algorithms, necessitating the development of quantum-resistant encryption methods.

Encryption's significance in cybersecurity is expected to grow as data plays a central role in digital interactions. Its effective use can thwart cybercriminals and nation-state actors, safeguard user privacy, and ensure the integrity of critical systems. As threats evolve, so too will encryption methods, with researchers continually developing new algorithms and protocols to stay ahead of potential vulnerabilities.

In conclusion, encryption is a cornerstone of cybersecurity, offering a robust means of protecting data from unauthorized access and ensuring its confidentiality, integrity, and authenticity. Understanding encryption's core principles, methods, and challenges is essential for individuals, organizations, and society at large as we navigate an increasingly digitized world. As cyber threats persist and technology advances, encryption will remain critical in the ongoing battle to secure the digital frontier.

CHAPTER V

Building a Cybersecurity Strategy

Developing a cybersecurity strategy

In today's increasingly digital and interconnected world, the importance of cybersecurity cannot be overstated. As organizations of all sizes and industries rely on technology to drive their operations and store sensitive data, a well- thought-out cybersecurity strategy is paramount. This section delves into the critical aspects of developing a cybersecurity strategy, emphasizing the importance of proactive measures, risk assessment, employee training, and incident response.

One of the fundamental principles of cybersecurity strategy development is the need for a proactive approach. Cyber threats are evolving alarmingly, with cybercriminals continually devising new and sophisticated methods to breach systems and steal data. Consequently, organizations must not wait for an attack to occur before taking action. Instead, they should adopt a proactive stance by continuously assessing and updating their cybersecurity measures. This entails staying current with the latest threats and vulnerabilities, regularly patching software and systems, and investing in cutting-edge security technologies.

Organizations must begin by conducting a comprehensive risk assessment to create an effective cybersecurity strategy. This entails determining which different assets— both digital and physical—need to be protected, as well as any potential threats or vulnerabilities that might allow these assets to be compromised. Organizations may focus their security efforts and direct resources where they are most needed by knowing the risks that are unique to them. This risk-based strategy guarantees the effectiveness and efficiency of cybersecurity operations by concentrating on the most important areas of concern.

In cybersecurity, human error is often cited as a significant contributing factor to breaches and incidents. Employees can unwittingly click on malicious links, fall victim to phishing attacks, or mishandle sensitive data. Therefore, any robust cybersecurity strategy should include a robust employee training program. Organizations can enable staff members to act as the first line of defense against cyberattacks by providing them with training on the most recent cybersecurity risks and best practices. This lowers the possibility of successful assaults and encourages cybersecurity knowledge across the entire organization.

In addition to prevention measures, organizations must also plan for the inevitable—cybersecurity incidents. No matter how strong the defenses, there is always a possibility that a breach may occur. Therefore, an incident response plan is a crucial component of any cybersecurity strategy. This plan outlines the steps to take when a security incident is detected, including how to contain the breach, investigate its scope and impact, and communicate with affected parties. An effective incident response plan minimizes the damage caused by an incident, reduces downtime, and helps maintain the organization's reputation.

While technology is significant in cybersecurity, it is essential to recognize that a successful strategy goes beyond just deploying the latest security tools. A holistic cybersecurity strategy encompasses people, processes, and technology. Effective cybersecurity governance and management processes are critical to ensure that security measures are aligned with the organization's goals and are consistently implemented. This entails defining clear roles and responsibilities for cybersecurity, establishing policies and procedures, and regularly monitoring and auditing security controls.

Furthermore, organizations must be prepared to adapt their cybersecurity strategy as the threat landscape evolves. Cyber threats are not static; new vulnerabilities and attack methods emerge regularly. Therefore, continuous improvement and agility are essential to an effective cybersecurity strategy. This involves conducting periodic reviews and assessments to identify improvement areas and adjust the strategy accordingly. Collaboration and information sharing are also crucial elements of a robust cybersecurity strategy.

Cybersecurity is not just an internal concern; it extends to the broader ecosystem in which organizations operate. Sharing threat intelligence and best practices with industry peers and government agencies can help organizations avoid emerging threats and enhance their overall cybersecurity posture.

In conclusion, developing a cybersecurity strategy is a multifaceted and ongoing process that demands careful consideration and proactive measures. Organizations must adopt a proactive approach, conduct thorough risk assessments, invest in employee training, and prepare for incidents through robust incident response plans. A holistic strategy encompassing people, processes, and technology is essential for long-term success.

Additionally, adapting to evolving threats and collaborating with others in the cybersecurity community is vital to staying resilient in the face of ever-changing cyber threats. By following these principles, organizations can significantly enhance their cybersecurity posture and protect their data, assets, and reputation in an increasingly digital world.

Risk assessment and risk management

In cybersecurity, the battle between cybercriminals and defenders is unceasing. With the growing dependence of organizations on digital technology and data, the stakes are higher than ever. Cyber threats are serious, and the consequences from a successful breach may be disastrous, resulting in everything from monetary losses to reputational harm to a company. This section explores the critical concepts of risk assessment and risk management in cybersecurity, emphasizing their role in identifying vulnerabilities, making informed decisions, and fortifying an organization's defenses against the ever- evolving threat landscape.

At the heart of effective cybersecurity lies risk assessment. In essence, risk assessment is the process of identifying, evaluating, and prioritizing potential vulnerabilities and threats within an organization's information systems and infrastructure. This entails comprehensively examining assets, including data, hardware, software, and network components, to determine their criticality to the organization's operations. Simultaneously, it involves assessing the likelihood and potential impact of various threats, including cyberattacks, data breaches, and system failures.

Central to risk assessment is the concept of risk analysis, which involves quantifying the identified risks. This often requires assigning numerical values to an incident's probability and potential impact. Combining these factors yields a risk score, which assists in prioritizing risks for mitigation efforts. Organizations can better understand their vulnerabilities and the possible consequences of security incidents by conducting risk assessments. This gives them the information they need to decide how best to safeguard their assets and where to allocate their resources.

Once risks have been identified and assessed, the next crucial step in the cybersecurity journey is risk management. Risk management implements strategies and measures to mitigate, accept, transfer, or avoid the identified risks. In essence, it is the action plan organizations put in place to protect their assets and reduce their exposure to cyber threats.

A basic principle of risk management is the concept of risk appetite. This refers to an organization's willingness to accept or tolerate certain levels of risk. Organizations may have varying risk appetites based on their industry, regulatory environment, and overall business objectives. Understanding and defining this risk appetite is essential as it guides decision-making throughout the risk management process.

Risk mitigation strategies are at the core of risk management. These strategies involve implementing security controls and measures to minmize the likelihood and impact of identified risks. Mitigation measures may encompass technical safeguards such as intrusion detection systems, firewalls, and encryption, as well as procedural safeguards like access controls and employee training programs. These measures aim to strengthen an organization's cybersecurity posture and make it more resilient to threats.

A critical aspect of mitigation strategies is the concept of defense-in-depth. This approach involves layering multiple security controls throughout an organization's IT infrastructure. The idea is to create numerous barriers that an attacker must overcome, increasing the complexity of successful breaches. A well-implemented defense-in-depth strategy reduces the organization's reliance on any single security control and enhances overall security.

Not all risks can be fully mitigated; some may be deemed acceptable based on an organization's risk appetite. In such cases, organizations choose to accept these risks, acknowledging that they exist but are manageable within established parameters. However, it is essential to document the acceptance of risks and regularly review them to ensure they remain within acceptable levels.

Alternatively, organizations may opt to transfer certain risks through insurance or contractual agreements. Cyber insurance has become increasingly popular, providing financial protection in case of a security breach or data loss. However, it is essential to recognize that insurance is not a replacement for robust cybersecurity practices; it should complement an organization's risk management efforts.

Effective risk management is an ongoing process. The cybersecurity landscape constantly evolves, with new threats and vulnerabilities emerging regularly. Consequently, organizations must continuously monitor their risk landscape, reassess their risks, and adapt their risk management strategies accordingly.

This involves staying abreast of the latest threat intelligence, monitoring the effectiveness of existing security controls, and adjusting risk management strategies as needed. Additionally, regular audits and assessments help ensure an organization's risk management practices align with its evolving business environment.

In the digital era, successful cybersecurity requires both risk assessment and risk management. Organizations must proactively identify and assess vulnerabilities and threats, quantify the associated risks, and implement mitigation strategies that are in line with their risk appetite and business objectives. This proactive approach strengthens an organization's defenses against cyber threats and helps protect its reputation, customer trust, and bottom line. Furthermore, recognizing that cybersecurity is an ever-changing landscape, organizations that continuously monitor and adapt their risk management practices will be better positioned to navigate the evolving threat landscape and emerge resilient in the face of cyber adversaries.

Incident response planning

In the ever-evolving world of cybersecurity, incidents such as data breaches and cyberattacks have become inevitable. Responding swiftly and effectively to these incidents is critical to minimize damage, protect sensitive data, and maintain an organization's reputation. This section delves into the importance of incident response planning in cybersecurity, highlighting its key components, and emphasizing its role in reducing the impact of security breaches.

Incident response planning is the proactive process of preparing for, managing, and mitigating the aftermath of cybersecurity incidents. It is a structured and well-documented approach to handling incidents, whether from external threats or internal vulnerabilities. The primary goal of incident response planning is to minimize the impact of security incidents, including data breaches, system compromises, and malware infections, by swiftly containing the incident, investigating its scope, and implementing measures to prevent future occurrences.

One of the fundamental components of incident response planning is creating an incident response team. This team comprises individuals with specific roles and responsibilities, including incident coordinators, investigators, and communication liaisons. Having a well-defined team ensures that there is a clear chain of command and accountability during an incident. Training and regular drills are essential to keep the response team prepared and knowledgeable about the latest threats and incident response procedures.

The incident response plan should also include predefined procedures for identifying, classifying, and reporting incidents. This involves establishing criteria for determining the severity of an incident and its possible impact on the organization. Incident classification helps prioritize responses and allocate resources effectively. Equally important is establishing clear communication channels both within the organization and with external stakeholders, like customers, law enforcement, and regulatory bodies. Effective communication is crucial for managing the incident's fallout and maintaining transparency.

In the event of an incident, the incident response team's first task is containment. Containment involves isolating the affected systems or networks to prevent further damage and unauthorized access. This step often requires technical expertise to ensure that the incident does not spread. Rapid containment can significantly reduce the extent of the breach and limit its impact on the organization.

Once containment is achieved, the incident response team proceeds with an investigation to determine the scope and nature of the incident. This involves gathering evidence, analyzing logs, and comprehending the TTPs (tactics, techniques, and procedures) employed by the attackers. A thorough investigation is crucial for understanding the incident and strengthening the organization's defenses against future attacks.

Simultaneously, the incident response plan should outline strategies for eradicating the root causes of the incident. This may involve patching vulnerabilities, removing malware, and implementing additional security measures to prevent a recurrence. Lessons learned from the incident should be documented and used to enhance the organization's overall cybersecurity posture.

Post-incident activities are also a critical part of the response plan. These activities include notifying affected parties, such as customers, partners, and regulators, about the incident and its impact. Transparency and timely communication are essential to maintaining trust and credibility. Additionally, organizations may need to comply with legal and regulatory requirements, like data breach notification laws, which may vary depending on the jurisdiction and industry.

Finally, a crucial aspect of incident response planning is the post-incident review and continuous improvement process. After the incident has been addressed, the incident response team should thoroughly review the incident response process. This includes an assessment of what worked well and what could be improved. The goal is to identify areas for enhancement and refine the incident response plan based on the lessons learned.

In conclusion, incident response planning is an indispensable component of cybersecurity strategy. It provides organizations with a structured and proactive approach to managing and reducing the impact of cybersecurity incidents. By establishing a dedicated incident response team, defining clear procedures, and emphasizing swift containment, investigation, and communication, organizations can effectively minimize the damage caused by security breaches. Furthermore, the post-incident review and continuous improvement process ensure that the organization's incident response capabilities evolve in step with the ever-changing threat landscape. Ultimately, a well-executed incident response plan is essential for maintaining cybersecurity resilience in the face of growing cyber threats.

Security policies and employee training

In the digital age, where data breaches and cyberattacks are pervasive, organizations must place cybersecurity at the forefront of their operations. While advanced technologies and robust security tools are critical components of a comprehensive cybersecurity strategy, the role of security policies and employee training should not be underestimated. This section explores the significance of security policies and employee training in cybersecurity, highlighting how they shape organizational defenses, enhance security awareness, and mitigate the ever-evolving cyber threats.

Security policies are the foundation of any effective cybersecurity program. They serve as guidelines, principles, and rules that dictate how an organization should protect its information assets, systems, and networks. These policies encompass many areas, including data protection, access control, incident response, and acceptable use of technology resources. Security policies provide a framework for defining security objectives and aligning them with the organization's goals and regulatory requirements.

One of the primary functions of security policies is to establish a standardized and consistent approach to security across the organization. They define the duties and responsibilities of employees and specify the security controls and measures that should be implemented. By creating a clear framework, security policies help organizations maintain consistency in their security practices, reducing the risk of vulnerabilities caused by ad-hoc or inconsistent security measures.

Moreover, security policies play a crucial role in compliance and risk management. Many industries and jurisdictions have strict regulatory requirements for data protection and security. Security policies help organizations ensure compliance with these regulations by providing a documented roadmap for addressing security-related concerns. In an audit or breach, well-documented security policies can demonstrate an organization's commitment to security and its efforts to adhere with relevant laws and standards.

However, the mere existence of security policies is not enough. Organizations must frequently review and update their policies to reflect changes in the threat and technology landscape. Cyber threats evolve rapidly, and policies that were effective in the past may no longer suffice. Continuous improvement of security policies is essential to address emerging risks and vulnerabilities effectively.

While security policies set the framework for cybersecurity practices, they are only effective if employees understand and adhere to them. This is where employee training becomes indispensable. Employee training programs educate staff about security policies, best practices, and the latest cybersecurity threats. They empower employees to recognize and respond to security incidents and make them an integral part of the organization's defense against cyber threats.

One of the main objectives of employee training is to raise security awareness among the workforce. Many cybersecurity incidents result from human error, such as clicking on phishing emails or inadvertently sharing sensitive information. Organizations can significantly mitigate the risk of these incidents by offering employees with the knowledge and skills to identify potential threats and make informed security decisions.

Training also helps employees comprehend their role in maintaining the organization's cybersecurity posture. They learn how to handle sensitive data securely, follow access control procedures, and report suspicious activities. This reduces the likelihood of breaches and fosters a culture of awareness in cybersecurity throughout the organization.

Furthermore, employee training programs are instrumental in preparing staff for incident response. In case of a security incident, the ability of employees to follow predefined procedures and cooperate with the incident response team is critical. Training ensures that employees know what to do, whom to contact, and how to assist during an incident, which can significantly improve the organization's response time and effectiveness.

Effective employee training should be an ongoing process. Cyber threats are continuously evolving, and new attack vectors emerge regularly. Therefore, organizations must provide continuous training and updates to inform employees about the latest threats and best practices. This includes conducting simulated phishing exercises, security drills, and regular security awareness campaigns to reinforce the importance of cybersecurity.

Organizations should integrate their security policies and employee training efforts to achieve the most robust cybersecurity posture. Security policies should be a central component of employee training programs, ensuring that employees understand the policies and know how to apply them in their day-to-day work. Additionally, training programs should emphasize the importance of compliance with security policies and the consequences of non-compliance.

Furthermore, organizations can use training to reinforce specific security policies and practices. For example, training modules can focus on data protection, secure password management, and recognizing social engineering tactics. By aligning training content with the organization's security policies, organizations can ensure that employees are well-prepared to implement these policies effectively.

In conclusion, security policies and employee training are essential to an effective cybersecurity strategy. Security policies provide the framework and guidelines for protecting information assets, while employee training programs empower staff to understand and adhere to these policies. Integrating security policies and training efforts fosters a culture of cybersecurity awareness and preparedness, reducing the risk of security incidents and enhancing an organization's resilience against the ever-evolving cyber threat landscape. In today's digital landscape, organizations prioritizing security policies and employee training are better positioned to defend against cyber threats and safeguard their valuable data and assets.

CHAPTER VI

Ethical Hacking Methodology

The steps in ethical hacking

Ethical hacking, known as penetration testing or white-hat hacking, intentionally probes computer systems, networks, and applications to uncover vulnerabilities and weaknesses. Ethical hacking aims to help organizations identify and rectify security flaws before malicious hackers can exploit them. To conduct successful ethical hacking, security professionals follow a well-structured series of steps that ensure a comprehensive assessment of an organization's cybersecurity posture. This section will delve into the key steps involved in ethical hacking.

The initial step in ethical hacking is meticulous planning and preparation. Ethical hackers need a clear understanding of the target system, including its architecture, technology stack, and potential vulnerabilities. They also need to define the scope of the engagement, specifying what systems and networks are within the scope of the assessment and what is off-limits. This stage involves setting clear objectives, obtaining any necessary permissions or authorizations, and assembling the required tools and resources.

Information gathering is a critical phase of ethical hacking. It involves collecting as much information as possible about the target organization, including its network infrastructure, web applications, and employees. This information can be gathered through open-source intelligence (OSINT), network scanning, and social engineering. The goal is to understand the target environment and identify potential entry points comprehensively.

Once the information gathering phase is complete, ethical hackers analyze the collected data to identify potential vulnerabilities and weaknesses in the target systems. This analysis includes assessing the configuration of systems, examining software versions, and searching for known vulnerabilities that could be exploited.

Ethical hackers try to use the vulnerabilities they have found to their advantage in order to access the target systems without authorization during the exploitation phase. This step may involve techniques, including leveraging known exploits, conducting privilege escalation, or manipulating input data to trigger vulnerabilities. The objective is to demonstrate the potential impact of these vulnerabilities and assess how an attacker could exploit them.

After successfully gaining access to a system, ethical hackers continue to assess its security by performing post-exploitation activities. This phase involves maintaining access to the compromised system, conducting further reconnaissance, and escalating privileges to see the extent of potential damage a malicious attacker could cause.

Accurate documentation is a crucial aspect of ethical hacking. Ethical hackers must maintain detailed records of their actions, findings, and any potential security risks they uncover throughout the engagement. This documentation creates a comprehensive report outlining the vulnerabilities discovered, their potential impact, and recommended remediation measures. This report is then provided to the organization's stakeholders, such as IT teams and management, to guide the process of addressing and fixing the identified security issues.

The final step in ethical hacking is the remediation and follow-up phase. Once the organization receives the ethical hacking report, it addresses the identified vulnerabilities and implements security improvements. Ethical hackers often work closely with the organization during this phase to provide guidance and verify that the recommended fixes are effective. Regular follow-up assessments may also be conducted to ensure the organization's cybersecurity posture is continuously improving.

In conclusion, ethical hacking is crucial in helping organizations proactively identify and address cybersecurity vulnerabilities. By following a well-defined series of steps, ethical hackers can systematically assess an organization's security posture, uncover weaknesses, and provide actionable recommendations for improvement. Ethical hacking is a valuable tool for enhancing security and an essential practice in an era where cyber threats continue to evolve and pose significant risks to organizations worldwide.

Reconnaissance and information gathering

Reconnaissance and information gathering are foundational stages in cybersecurity, where knowledge is power. These initial phases are critical for offensive and defensive purposes, as they allow security professionals to understand their systems better and identify potential vulnerabilities. This section delves into the significance of reconnaissance and information gathering in cybersecurity, highlighting their role in threat intelligence, risk assessment, and the protection of digital assets.

Reconnaissance is the process of collecting information about a target, be it an individual, an organization, or a network, to gain insights that can be leveraged for various purposes. In the context of cybersecurity, reconnaissance plays a pivotal role in understanding the landscape in which cyber threats and attacks operate.

One of the primary goals of reconnaissance is threat intelligence gathering. Cyber threats constantly evolve, with new attack vectors and tactics emerging regularly. Organizations must actively collect and analyze information about potential adversaries, their motivations, and capabilities to avoid these threats. This includes monitoring online forums and communities where threat actors congregate, tracking malware campaigns, and analyzing indicators of compromise (IoCs) to identify potential security risks.

Moreover, reconnaissance is instrumental in risk assessment. Organizations need to understand their vulnerabilities and weaknesses before developing a robust cybersecurity strategy. This involves collecting data on the organization's assets, such as servers, applications, and data repositories, and assessing their exposure to potential threats. Reconnaissance can help organizations identify potential attack routes and vulnerabilities so they can allocate resources and prioritize security activities.

On the other hand, information gathering focuses on obtaining specific details about a target, often in preparation for an attack or a security assessment. This phase is typically more tactical and involves gathering data related to network configurations, software versions, open ports, and potential vulnerabilities.

One common technique in information gathering is network scanning. Security professionals use specialized tools to scan target networks and systems to identify open ports, services running on those ports, and the operating systems in use. This information helps attackers pinpoint potential entry points and vulnerabilities that may be exploited.

Footprinting is another aspect of information gathering. It involves collecting data about an organization's online presence, such as its website, domain registrations, and public records. Attackers use footprinting to identify employees, their roles, and contact details. This information can be valuable for launching targeted attacks, such as phishing campaigns.

It is essential to emphasize that both reconnaissance and information gathering can serve ethical and malicious purposes. Ethical hackers, also known as white-hat hackers, conduct these activities with the consent and authorization of the target organization to identify and remediate vulnerabilities. Malicious actors, conversely, perform reconnaissance and information gathering to launch cyberattacks intending to compromise systems and steal sensitive data.

In cybersecurity defense, organizations must proactively defend against reconnaissance and information gathering techniques. This involves implementing intrusion detection systems (IDS) and intrusion prevention systems (IPS) that can detect and block scanning activities. Additionally, organizations should regularly conduct reconnaissance and information gathering activities to identify and address their vulnerabilities before malicious actors do.

In conclusion, reconnaissance and information gathering are foundational stages in the complex landscape of cybersecurity. They play a pivotal role in threat intelligence, risk assessment, and the protection of digital assets. Security professionals and organizations alike must recognize the dual nature of these activities, where ethical reconnaissance is used to fortify defenses, while malicious information gathering poses a significant cybersecurity threat. To maintain robust security postures in an ever-evolving digital world, proactive defense against reconnaissance and information gathering is essential.

Vulnerability assessment

In the ever-evolving landscape of cybersecurity, organizations face an ongoing battle against many threats and vulnerabilities that could compromise their digital assets and data. Vulnerability assessment, a methodical and proactive technique to locating and resolving vulnerabilities in an organization's IT systems and infrastructure, is an essential part of a comprehensive cybersecurity strategy. This section explores the significance of vulnerability assessment, highlighting its role in risk reduction, proactive defense, and regulatory compliance.

Vulnerability assessment systematically identifies and evaluates vulnerabilities within an organization's IT systems, networks, and applications. The primary objective is to discover potential weaknesses that cybercriminals and malicious actors could exploit. These vulnerabilities may stem from misconfigurations, outdated software, weak access controls, or other security flaws.

One of the fundamental benefits of vulnerability assessment is its contribution to risk reduction. By proactively identifying vulnerabilities, organizations can take steps to remediate them before they are exploited. This significantly reduces the organization's exposure to potential cyber threats and the associated risks. Vulnerability assessment helps organizations prioritize their security efforts by focusing on the most critical vulnerabilities that pose the highest risk.

Furthermore, vulnerability assessment plays a crucial role in proactive defense. In the cybersecurity landscape, organizations cannot solely rely on reactive measures like incident response when breaches occur. Vulnerability assessment is the foundation of proactive defense, which helps organizations stay a step ahead of cyber threats. It allows for identifying and mitigating vulnerabilities before attackers can capitalize on them. This approach reduces the organization's attack surface and strengthens its overall cybersecurity posture.

Organizations typically use automated scanning tools that scan their IT infrastructure for known vulnerabilities to conduct effective vulnerability assessments. These tools compare the system's configuration and software versions against a database of known vulnerabilities and generate reports detailing the findings. While automated scanning is a valuable initial step, it must be complemented with manual testing and analysis. Skilled security professionals can identify vulnerabilities that automated tools might miss, such as logical flaws or configuration issues.

Moreover, vulnerability assessment plays a significant role in regulatory compliance. Many industries and jurisdictions have specific cybersecurity regulations and compliance requirements. Vulnerability assessment is often a mandatory component of these regulations. Organizations can demonstrate their commitment to adherence and avoid potential legal and financial consequences by conducting regular assessments and addressing identified vulnerabilities.

It is crucial to recognize that vulnerability assessment is an ongoing process. Cyber threats are always evolving, and new vulnerabilities emerge regularly. Thus, organizations must conduct regular and periodic vulnerability assessments to maintain an up-to-date understanding of their security posture. This includes scanning externally facing systems and internal networks and applications, which are often overlooked but can still pose significant risks.

In conclusion, vulnerability assessment is critical to any robust cybersecurity strategy. It empowers organizations to proactively identify and address weaknesses in their IT systems, reducing the risk of cyber threats and potential data breaches. Vulnerability assessment fosters a culture of proactive defense, allowing organizations to stay ahead of cyber adversaries. Moreover, it helps organizations comply with cybersecurity regulations and standards, demonstrating their commitment to data security. In today's digital landscape, where cyber threats are ubiquitous, vulnerability assessment is an indispensable tool to protect digital assets and maintain a resilient cybersecurity posture.

Exploitation and penetration

Exploitation and penetration testing represent the culmination of ethical hacking practices, where security professionals simulate real-world cyberattacks to assess an organization's vulnerability to malicious actors. These phases are pivotal components of a comprehensive cybersecurity strategy, enabling organizations to identify weaknesses, assess potential risks, and reinforce their defenses. This section explores the significance of exploitation and penetration testing, highlighting their role in evaluating security postures, uncovering vulnerabilities, and fostering proactive defense.

Exploitation, in the context of ethical hacking, involves attempting to leverage identified vulnerabilities to gain unauthorized access or control over a target system or network. The primary objective is to illustrate the potential consequences of these vulnerabilities and highlight their potential impact on an organization. Exploitation goes beyond merely identifying weaknesses; it provides concrete evidence of their risks.

Ethical hackers often use various techniques during the exploitation phase to validate the presence and severity of vulnerabilities. These may include leveraging known exploits, manipulating input data to trigger vulnerabilities, or attempting privilege escalation to gain greater control over a compromised system. The goal is to replicate the actions that a malicious attacker might take to compromise an organization's assets.

Once successful exploitation occurs, the process often transitions into penetration testing. Penetration testing is a broader evaluation of an organization's security defenses, simulating a cyberattack from initial reconnaissance to full compromise. Unlike exploitation, which focuses on specific vulnerabilities, penetration testing encompasses a more extensive assessment of an organization's overall cybersecurity posture.

The penetration testing process typically follows a structured methodology that includes information gathering, vulnerability identification, exploitation, post-exploitation, and reporting. This approach allows ethical hackers to identify and assess vulnerabilities throughout the attack chain, from initial reconnaissance to potential data exfiltration.

One of the primary advantages of exploitation and penetration testing is the ability to provide organizations with a realistic and actionable assessment of their security postures. Rather than presenting abstract lists of vulnerabilities, ethical hackers demonstrate how these vulnerabilities can be exploited and the potential consequences of such exploitation. This tangible evidence is invaluable for organizations to understand the urgency of remediation and prioritizing security efforts.

Furthermore, exploitation and penetration testing facilitate proactive defense. By uncovering vulnerabilities and potential attack vectors, organizations can take proactive measures to improve their defenses before malicious actors can exploit them. This includes implementing security patches, enhancing access controls, and fortifying network configurations. Ultimately, the goal is to reduce an organization's attack surface and minimize the danger of successful cyberattacks.

It is crucial to highlight that exploitation and penetration testing should only be conducted with the full consent and authorization of the target organization. Unauthorized testing can lead to legal and ethical complications, and organizations must ensure that they have proper agreements in place with the ethical hacking team. Ethical hackers adhere to strict codes of conduct and operate within legal boundaries to maintain the trust and integrity of the security profession.

In conclusion, exploitation and penetration testing are integral components of an organization's cybersecurity strategy. They provide a realistic assessment of security vulnerabilities, demonstrate their potential impact, and facilitate proactive defense measures. By simulating cyberattacks and identifying weaknesses in security defenses, organizations can take meaningful steps to fortify their cybersecurity postures and protect their digital assets. In an age where cyber threats are a constant concern, ethical hacking practices like exploitation and penetration testing are indispensable for maintaining robust and resilient cybersecurity defenses.

Reporting and remediation

Reporting and remediation are crucial stages in the ethical hacking and vulnerability assessment process, where the insights gained from testing and assessments are transformed into actionable recommendations for enhancing an organization's cybersecurity defenses. These phases bridge the gap between identifying vulnerabilities and implementing measures to mitigate them, which is pivotal in fortifying an organization's security posture. This section delves into the significance of reporting and remediation, highlighting their role in risk reduction, decision-making, and continuous improvement.

Reporting in ethical hacking serves as the formal documentation of the findings and insights gathered throughout the assessment or penetration testing process. It is the mechanism through which ethical hackers communicate their discoveries to the organization's stakeholders, including IT teams, management, and decision-makers. The primary goal of reporting is to provide a comprehensive and clear understanding of the identified vulnerabilities and their potential impact.

The ethical hacking report typically includes detailed information about each vulnerability, such as its nature, severity, potential consequences, and the methods used for exploitation. Reports may also include recommendations for remediation, which serve as a roadmap for addressing the identified vulnerabilities. These recommendations are typically prioritized based on the vulnerabilities' severity and potential impact on the organization's operations and security.

The remediation phase follows the reporting stage and involves the organization taking action to address and mitigate the identified vulnerabilities. Remediation activities can encompass various measures, including applying security patches, configuring security controls, enhancing access controls, and implementing new security technologies. The goal is to reduce the organization's exposure to potential cyber threats and strengthen its overall cybersecurity posture.

Effective reporting and remediation have several significant benefits for organizations. One of the key advantages is risk reduction. Once identified and understood through reporting, vulnerabilities can be promptly addressed through remediation efforts. This reduces the organization's exposure to potential threats and lowers the likelihood of successful cyberattacks. Risk reduction is particularly critical in industries with strict regulatory requirements and compliance standards.

Moreover, reporting and remediation support informed decision-making. Ethical hacking reports provide organizations with valuable insights into their cybersecurity strengths and weaknesses. Armed with this knowledge, decision-makers can make informed choices regarding resource allocation, budgeting, and the prioritization of security initiatives. The actionable recommendations in reports guide organizations in developing strategies to enhance their security posture effectively.

Continuous improvement is another significant benefit of reporting and remediation. Cyber threats and vulnerabilities constantly evolve, requiring organizations to adapt and refine their security defenses continuously. Ethical hacking reports serve as a foundation for ongoing security improvement efforts. Organizations can use these reports as a basis for periodic security assessments, audits, and updates to their security policies and procedures.

The effectiveness of reporting and remediation processes depends on clear and open communication between ethical hackers and the organization's internal teams. Collaboration is essential to ensure the recommended remediation measures are correctly understood and implemented. Ethical hackers often work closely with IT teams and security personnel to validate the effectiveness of remediation efforts and verify that vulnerabilities have been successfully addressed.

In conclusion, reporting and remediation are indispensable components of a proactive and resilient cybersecurity strategy. They transform the insights gained from ethical hacking assessments into actionable recommendations and tangible improvements to an organization's security posture. By reducing risk, facilitating informed decision-making, and promoting continuous improvement, reporting and remediation empower organizations to stay ahead of developing cyber threats and safeguard their digital assets and data. In an era where cybersecurity is a top priority, these processes are essential for organizations seeking to maintain robust and resilient defenses against cyber adversaries.

CHAPTER VII

Penetration Testing Techniques

Detailed explanation of penetration testing

Penetration testing, often called pen testing or ethical hacking, is a proactive and systematic approach to assessing an organization's cybersecurity defenses. It simulates real-world cyberattacks to uncover vulnerabilities and weaknesses that malicious actors could exploit.

The primary objectives of penetration testing are to identify vulnerabilities and assess an organization's security posture. By simulating cyberattacks, penetration testers aim to discover weaknesses in an organization's systems, networks, applications, and configurations. These vulnerabilities may include software bugs, misconfigurations, weak access controls, and other security flaws. Additionally, the testing process assesses the effectiveness of existing security controls, such as intrusion detection systems, firewalls, and access controls. It helps organizations determine whether these measures adequately protect against potential threats and measure compliance with cybersecurity standards, regulatory requirements, and best practices.

Penetration testing can be categorized into various methodologies tailored to specific objectives and scenarios. In black box testing, the ethical hacker operates with minimal prior knowledge of the target environment, simulating an external threat actor with little to no internal information. On the other hand, white box testing takes the opposite approach, where testers have full knowledge of the target systems, including access to source code, system configurations, and network diagrams. Gray box testing combines black box and white box testing elements, with testers possessing partial knowledge of the target environment, striking a balance between external and internal perspectives.

The benefits of penetration testing for organizations are manifold. Firstly, it helps identify vulnerabilities that may go undetected by automated scanning tools or traditional security assessments. Secondly, it provides realistic insights into how an organization's defenses stand up against potential cyber threats, aiding organizations in prioritizing remediation efforts effectively. Thirdly, organizations can reduce their risk of falling victim to cyberattacks and data breaches by addressing identified vulnerabilities. Lastly, penetration testing can assist organizations in meeting regulatory compliance requirements by providing detailed reports demonstrating a commitment to security.

The penetration testing process typically follows a structured methodology. It begins with planning, where the test's scope, goals, and objectives are defined, and necessary permissions and authorizations are obtained. Next comes the reconnaissance phase, where testers gather information about the target environment through various means. This is followed by vulnerability analysis, which analyzes the collected information to identify potential vulnerabilities and weaknesses. In the exploitation phase, testers attempt to exploit identified vulnerabilities to gain illegal access or control over target systems. After access is achieved, the post-exploitation phase assesses the potential impact of a successful attack. Finally, the findings and insights are documented in a comprehensive report, including identified vulnerabilities, potential impact, and recommended remediation measures. Organizations then take action to address and mitigate identified vulnerabilities, with ethical hackers often providing guidance and verification of remediation efforts.

In conclusion, penetration testing is a vital component of modern cybersecurity practices. It offers organizations with a proactive approach to identifying and addressing vulnerabilities, helping them strengthen their security posture, reduce risks, and safeguard their digital assets and data in an increasingly challenging threat landscape.

Types of penetration testing (e.g., black box, white box, gray box)

Penetration testing, a fundamental component of cybersecurity, simulates real-world cyberattacks to evaluate an organization's security defenses. Different types of penetration testing approaches are employed, each offering unique perspectives and insights into an organization's security posture. These types include black box testing, white box testing, and gray box testing. This section explores each penetration testing type's characteristics, methodologies, and applications, highlighting their roles in assessing vulnerabilities and enhancing cybersecurity.

Black box testing, also known as external testing or blind testing, simulates an attacker with little or no prior knowledge of the target environment. In this approach, the ethical hacker operates without access to internal network documentation, source code, or system architecture details. Black box testers rely on publicly available information and perform reconnaissance like a real attacker.

Black box testing mimics an external threat actor attempting to exploit vulnerabilities from an external perspective, such as through a public-facing website or network perimeter. It helps organizations understand how their systems withstand external threats, including common attack vectors like SQL injection, cross-site scripting (XSS), and network scanning.

White box testing, often called clear-box testing, glass-box testing, or complete disclosure testing, takes the opposite approach. In this methodology, the ethical hacker has comprehensive understanding of the internal workings of the target systems, including access to source code, network diagrams, and system configurations. White box testers typically work closely with internal IT and development teams.

White box testing provides an internal perspective, closely resembling the knowledge and access levels of an organization's IT staff. This approach is highly effective for assessing the security of application code, APIs, and configurations. It allows testers to uncover vulnerabilities deeply embedded within an organization's systems, making it an invaluable technique for strengthening application security and ensuring compliance with secure coding practices.

Gray box testing combines black box and white box testing elements, offering a middle-ground approach. Ethical hackers possess partial knowledge of the target environment in gray box testing. They may have limited access to system documentation, network diagrams, or application source code. This approach strikes a balance between external and internal perspectives.

Gray box testing is beneficial when simulating insider threats or attackers who may have gained partial access to an organization's systems, such as through compromised user credentials. By leveraging partial knowledge, gray box testers can assess the effectiveness of access controls, privilege escalation, and lateral movement within an organization's network.

Each type of penetration testing has its strengths and weaknesses, making them suitable for different scenarios and objectives. The choice of testing type depends on factors such as the organization's goals, the specific systems or applications under assessment, and the desired level of realism in the test. A well-rounded cybersecurity strategy often incorporates a mix of these testing types to evaluate an organization's security posture comprehensively.

In conclusion, penetration testing is critical in identifying and mitigating vulnerabilities within an organization's systems and applications. The three main types of penetration testing—black box, white box, and gray box—offer distinct perspectives and insights into an organization's security defenses. Black box testing provides an external, blind assessment, while white box testing offers an internal, full-disclosure examination. Gray box testing balance the two. By leveraging these testing types strategically, organizations can proactively address security weaknesses, reduce risks, and bolster their cybersecurity resilience in an era where cyber threats continue to evolve.

Tools and methodologies used in penetration testing

Penetration testing, a critical facet of modern cybersecurity, relies on a diverse toolkit and structured methodologies to simulate real-world cyberattacks and comprehensively assess an organization's security defenses. These tools and methodologies are the cornerstone of ethical hacking, aiding professionals in identifying vulnerabilities, evaluating security controls, and guiding organizations in prioritizing remediation efforts.

In the arsenal of penetration testers, tools play a pivotal role in scanning, probing, and exploiting potential weaknesses. Vulnerability scanners, such as Nessus and Qualys, automate the process of identifying known vulnerabilities within an organization's network or systems. Exploitation frameworks, like Metasploit, provide a controlled environment for ethical hackers to develop, test, and execute exploit code against vulnerabilities. Network scanners such as Nmap and Wireshark are instrumental in mapping networks, identifying open ports, and profiling target systems. Password cracking tools like John the Ripper and Hydra assess the strength of authentication mechanisms by attempting to crack passwords through various techniques. Specialized tools, like Burp Suite and OWASP ZAP, focus on web application penetration testing, detecting vulnerabilities like the SQL injection and cross-site scripting (XSS). For wireless network security, tools like Aircrack-ng and Reaver assess vulnerabilities in Wi-Fi networks. Additionally, the Social Engineering Toolkit (SET) aids in simulating social engineering attacks, evaluating an organization's susceptibility to techniques like phishing and credential harvesting.

Complementing these tools are structured methodologies that guide the penetration testing process. OWASP or Open Web Application Security Project methodology is a widely adopted framework for testing web applications, offering comprehensive coverage of vulnerabilities. The Penetration Testing Execution Standard (PTES) defines a holistic approach, from pre-engagement activities to reporting, providing a structured methodology for security testing. NIST, also known as National Institute of Standards and Technology, offers SP 800-115, a guideline document that outlines security testing and assessment processes. Information Systems Security Assessment Framework (ISSAF) is specifically tailored for assessing information systems and includes phases such as reconnaissance and exploitation. Lastly, the Open Source Security Testing Methodology Manual (OSSTMM) emphasizes quantifying risks and vulnerabilities, making it valuable for risk assessment.

The effectiveness of penetration testing often lies in the judicious combination of tools and methodologies. Ethical hackers select tools that align with the objectives of the assessment and apply methodologies appropriate to the scope of the test. For instance, a web application penetration test may employ tools like Burp Suite or OWASP ZAP while following the OWASP methodology to assess the application's security systematically. On the other hand, a network penetration test might utilize Nmap and Metasploit, guided by the PTES methodology to evaluate the security of an entire network.

Ultimately, the success of a penetration test hinges on the proficiency of ethical hackers in configuring, customizing, and interpreting tool outputs within the context of a structured methodology. This synergy between tools and methodologies empowers organizations to bolster their security posture, reduce risks, and safeguard their digital assets against evolving cyber threats. In a world where cybersecurity is a top priority, penetration testing is a critical safeguard for organizations, allowing them to proactively identify and remediate vulnerabilities before malicious actors can exploit them.

Real-world penetration testing examples

Penetration testing, often dubbed ethical hacking, is a practice that seeks to uncover security vulnerabilities by simulating real-world cyberattacks. In this section, we will explore several real-world penetration testing examples, showcasing how ethical hackers identify vulnerabilities, assess security controls, and help organizations fortify their defenses against a variety of threats.

A financial institution commissioned a penetration test of its online banking portal. Ethical hackers used web application scanning tools, like Burp Suite and OWASP ZAP, to identify potential vulnerabilities. They discovered a critical SQL injection flaw that could allow attackers to access sensitive customer data. By exploiting this vulnerability, the ethical hackers demonstrated how an attacker could manipulate the application's database. The findings prompted the organization to implement stringent input validation and security measures, preventing potential data breaches.

An e-commerce company engaged in a comprehensive network penetration test that included social engineering. Ethical hackers conducted reconnaissance to gather information about the organization's employees and systems. They then used this information to craft convincing phishing emails. They successfully tricked several employees into revealing their login credentials through these emails. This demonstrated the organization's susceptibility to social engineering attacks. Subsequent employee training and awareness programs were initiated to mitigate this risk.

A large retail chain sought to evaluate the security of its wireless networks across multiple store locations. Ethical hackers used tools like Aircrack-ng and Reaver to assess the Wi-Fi security protocols. In one store, they discovered that the network had weak encryption and lacked proper access controls. This vulnerability allowed unauthorized access to the network. The retail chain promptly upgraded its wireless security measures, implementing strong encryption and access controls to safeguard sensitive customer information.

A technology company opted for a red team engagement, where ethical hackers acted as external attackers attempting to compromise the organization's defenses. The red team conducted extensive reconnaissance, identified vulnerabilities in the perimeter firewall, and exploited them to gain initial access. They reached critical systems through lateral movement within the network, highlighting weaknesses in internal segmentation. The organization used these findings to reconfigure its network defenses, limit lateral movement, and enhance incident response procedures.

A healthcare provider engaged in penetration testing of its Internet of Things (IoT) medical devices. Ethical hackers examined the security of devices such as patient monitors and infusion pumps. They discovered that some devices lacked encryption for patient data transmission, making them susceptible to eavesdropping. Additionally, they identified default credentials hardcoded into some devices. The healthcare provider addressed these issues by applying encryption and implementing strong password policies for IoT devices, safeguarding patient information.

A cloud-based software-as-a-service (SaaS) provider conducted a penetration test of its infrastructure. Ethical hackers examined the security of the provider's cloud servers and applications. They identified misconfigurations in the cloud environment that could lead to data exposure and unauthorized access. The findings prompted the provider to reconfigure its cloud settings, implement multi-factor authentication, and regularly conduct security assessments to maintain a secure SaaS platform.

These real-world examples illustrate the versatility and significance of penetration testing in enhancing cybersecurity. Ethical hackers, armed with a wide array of tools and methodologies, uncover vulnerabilities, assess security controls, and provide organizations with actionable insights. By simulating real-world cyberattacks, organizations can proactively address weaknesses, reduce risks, and safeguard their digital assets in an ever-evolving threat landscape. In an era where cybersecurity is paramount, penetration testing remains an essential practice to ensure robust and resilient defenses against cyber threats.

CHAPTER VIII

Web Application Security

Common web application vulnerabilities

Web applications are a fundamental part of our digital lives, serving various purposes, from online banking to social media. However, their widespread use also makes them a prime target for cyberattacks. Common web application vulnerabilities pose significant risks to both users and organizations, potentially leading to data breaches, financial losses, and reputational damage. In this section, we will explore some of these vulnerabilities and understand their implications in the context of web security.

SQL Injection (SQLi) is a prevalent and severe web application vulnerability. It occurs when malicious users input crafted SQL queries into application forms or URL parameters. Attackers can use these queries to access, alter, or remove data from the database if the application fails to sufficiently sanitize or validate inputs. SQL injection can lead to data theft, data manipulation, or even a complete application compromise.

Another serious online vulnerability is called Cross-Site Scripting (XSS), and it involves inserting malicious scripts onto web sites that are being viewed by other users. Attackers can exploit this vulnerability to steal session cookies, redirect users to malicious websites, or deliver malware. XSS attacks come in several forms, including stored, reflected, and DOM-based XSS, each with its own consequences and exploitation methods.

Cross-Site Request Forgery (CSRF) attacks occur when an attacker tricks a user into making an unintentional and unauthorized request to a different site where the victim is authenticated. This can lead to actions being performed on the user's behalf without their consent, such as changing their account settings, initiating financial transactions, or altering data. CSRF vulnerabilities can have far-reaching consequences, especially in sensitive data or financial transactions applications.

Security misconfigurations involve improperly configured settings, such as default passwords, overly permissive access controls, or exposed sensitive information. These misconfigurations often result from oversight during development or deployment. Attackers can exploit them to obtain an unauthorized access to systems, escalate privileges, or glean valuable information about the application's architecture.

Broken authentication and session management vulnerabilities can lead to unauthorized access to user accounts. This can occur due to weak password policies, inadequate session management practices, or insufficient authentication mechanisms. Attackers can exploit these weaknesses to hijack user sessions, impersonate legitimate users, and gain unauthorized access to sensitive data or functionalities.

Insecure deserialization vulnerabilities arise when an application does not properly validate or sanitize data received from untrusted sources during deserialization processes. Attackers can utilize this vulnerability to execute arbitrary code, leading to remote code execution, data tampering, or denial-of-service attacks.

Insecure Direct Object References (IDOR) vulnerabilities occur when an attacker can manipulate object references to access unauthorized data or resources. This often happens when an application relies solely on user-supplied input for object reference, without proper access controls. Exploiting IDOR can result in data exposure, unauthorized access, or data manipulation.

Addressing these common web application vulnerabilities requires a multi-faceted approach that combines secure coding practices, regular security assessments, and the use of web application firewalls and security tools. Developers should implement input validation, output encoding, and secure authentication mechanisms. Security testing, including code reviews, static analysis, and dynamic scanning, can help identify vulnerabilities during development. Regular security audits and penetration testing are vital to uncover and remediate vulnerabilities in production environments.

In conclusion, common web application vulnerabilities pose significant threats to both users and organizations. These vulnerabilities can lead to data breaches, financial losses, and reputational damage. To mitigate these risks, developers and organizations must prioritize secure coding practices, conduct regular security assessments, and stay vigilant against emerging threats. In an interconnected digital world, robust web application security is essential for safeguarding sensitive data and maintaining user trust.

OWASP Top Ten vulnerabilities

The OWASP Top Ten is a widely recognized and respected list of the most critical web application security vulnerabilities. Compiled by the OWASP (Open Web Application Security Project), this list serves as a valuable resource for developers, security professionals, as well as organizations to understand and prioritize web application security risks. In this section, we will delve into each of the OWASP Top Ten vulnerabilities, exploring their characteristics, implications, and the importance of addressing them in the context of web security.

Injection vulnerabilities, like the SQL injection and command injection, occur when untrusted data is improperly handled and executed as part of a query or command. Attackers can exploit these vulnerabilities to manipulate databases, execute arbitrary code, and gain an unauthorized access to an application's resources. Proper input validation and parameterized queries are crucial to prevent injection attacks.

Broken authentication vulnerabilities result from weaknesses in user authentication and session management. Attackers can exploit these flaws to impersonate users, hijack sessions, or bypass authentication mechanisms. Implementing strong password policies, multi-factor authentication, and secure session management is essential to mitigate these risks.

Sensitive data exposure occurs when applications fail to protect confidential information, such as passwords or credit card details. Attackers can intercept, steal, or manipulate this data when it is inadequately secured. Encryption, secure storage, and robust access controls are vital safeguards against sensitive data exposure.

XML External Entity (XXE) vulnerabilities arise when an application parses XML input insecurely, allowing attackers to exploit external entities to retrieve confidential data, conduct denial-of-service attacks, or execute remote code. Properly configuring XML parsers and sanitizing input are essential to mitigate XXE risks.

Broken access control vulnerabilities exist when an application fails to enforce proper authorization and access controls. Attackers can exploit these weaknesses to access unauthorized functionalities or sensitive data. Implementing role-based access control and enforcing access controls on the server side is critical to prevent such breaches.

Security misconfigurations result from improperly configured settings, such as default passwords, overly permissive access controls, or exposed sensitive information. Attackers can exploit these misconfigurations to gain unauthorized access or glean valuable insights about the application's architecture. Regular audits and security assessments are necessary to detect and rectify security misconfigurations.

Cross-Site Scripting (XSS) vulnerabilities exist when an application allows untrusted data to be executed as scripts within a user's browser. Attackers can inject malicious scripts, steal cookies, or redirect users to phishing sites. Input validation, output encoding, and proper handling of user-generated content are essential measures to mitigate XSS risks.

Insecure deserialization vulnerabilities arise when an application improperly handles serialized data from untrusted sources. Attackers can carry out these vulnerabilities to execute arbitrary code, leading to remote code execution, data tampering, or denial-of-service attacks. Secure deserialization practices are essential to prevent such attacks.

Applications often rely on third-party components, libraries, or frameworks. Using outdated or vulnerable versions of these components can expose an application to known exploits. Regularly updating and patching these components and monitoring security advisories are essential to mitigate this risk.

Insufficient logging and monitoring can hinder an organization's ability to effectively identify and address security incidents. Attackers can exploit this lack of visibility to conduct unauthorized activities without detection. Robust logging, monitoring, and incident response procedures are critical for timely threat detection and mitigation.

Addressing the OWASP Top Ten vulnerabilities is paramount for organizations to bolster their web application security. A comprehensive approach includes secure coding practices, regular security assessments, patch management, and robust incident response capabilities. By prioritizing these vulnerabilities and implementing appropriate security measures, organizations can mitigate the risk of data breaches, financial losses, and reputational damage, ultimately safeguarding their web applications and protecting user trust in an increasingly connected digital landscape.

Techniques to secure web applications

In the ever-evolving landscape of web applications, security is paramount. The prevalence of online services and the value of the data they handle have made web applications prime targets for cyberattacks. Organizations must employ a multifaceted approach to secure their web applications to counter these threats and protect sensitive data. This section delves into various techniques crucial for ensuring web applications' robust security.

Secure coding practices are the cornerstone of web application security. Developers play a pivotal role in preventing common vulnerabilities by implementing best practices like input validation, output encoding, and proper error handling. Input validation ensures that user inputs are checked and sanitized, thereby mitigating risks associated with SQL injection and Cross-Site Scripting (XSS) attacks. Output encoding guarantees that user-generated content is displayed safely, reducing the risk of XSS vulnerabilities.

Additionally, developers can benefit from using security libraries and frameworks. These tools provide pre-built security functions that simplify the implementation of essential security controls. For example, the OWASP ESAPI library offers input validation and output encoding functions, helping developers adhere to security best practices. Using well-maintained frameworks like Spring Security for Java applications or Django for Python can significantly enhance security by incorporating built-in security features.

Web Application Firewalls (WAFs) serve as a protective barrier against potential threats. These solutions analyze incoming traffic, filtering out malicious requests and blocking common attack patterns such as SQL injection and XSS. Implementing a WAF as part of a defense-in-depth strategy provides an additional layer of protection, complementing other security measures.

Regular security assessments are essential for identifying and addressing security weaknesses. Penetration testing simulates real-world attacks, and automated vulnerability scanners can help uncover common vulnerabilities. Continuous monitoring and regular assessments are critical to maintaining a secure posture and adapting to evolving threats.

Authentication and authorization mechanisms are crucial for controlling user access. Strong authentication, including multi-factor authentication (MFA), adds a further layer of security by requiring users to provide multiple verification forms. Role-based access control ensures that users have appropriate permissions based on their roles and responsibilities.

Secure session management is paramount to prevent session hijacking and fixation attacks. Implementing secure cookies, employing session timeouts, and regenerating session identifiers upon login enhance security. Additionally, using secure channels (HTTPS) for all authenticated communication is vital to protect session data.

Data encryption, both in transit and at rest, safeguards sensitive information. Transport Layer Security (or TLS) or Secure Sockets Layer (or SSL) ensures data encryption during transmission. Encryption algorithms protect sensitive information stored in databases or on disk for data at rest.

Proper error handling is critical to prevent information leakage that could aid attackers. Implementing custom error messages and avoiding the exposure of sensitive system details to users enhance security. Effective logging and monitoring are also essential for promptly detecting and responding to security incidents. Monitoring logs for unusual activities and establishing an incident response plan ensure that security breaches are addressed effectively.

Content Security Policy (CSP) is a powerful feature that helps mitigate XSS attacks by specifying which scripts and resources a browser can load and execute. Defining a strict CSP can significantly reduce the risk of malicious scripts running within web applications.

Finally, organizations must prioritize patch management. Regularly updating and patching web application components, including third-party libraries and frameworks, is crucial. Outdated software often contains known vulnerabilities that attackers can exploit. Implementing a robust patch management process is essential to stay up-to-date with security fixes and maintain the security of web applications.

In conclusion, securing web applications requires a comprehensive and proactive approach. Organizations can significantly mitigate the risk of security breaches by adopting secure coding practices, leveraging security libraries, implementing web application firewalls, conducting regular security assessments, and following robust authentication, authorization, and encryption practices. Effective session management, error handling, logging, and content security policies further bolster an application's defenses. These techniques collectively ensure that web applications remain resilient against evolving threats, safeguarding sensitive data, user privacy, and organizational reputation in today's digital age.

The importance of secure coding practices

In today's interconnected digital world, secure coding practices are not merely desirable; they are a fundamental necessity. The ubiquitous use of software in various aspects of our lives, from online banking to healthcare management, has made the security of software applications paramount. Secure coding practices are at the forefront of this endeavor, serving as the bedrock upon which robust cybersecurity is built. This section explores the critical significance of secure coding practices, elucidating their pivotal role in mitigating vulnerabilities, safeguarding data, and fostering trust in software systems.

First and foremost, secure coding practices are instrumental in mitigating vulnerabilities that malicious actors could exploit. By adhering to industry-recognized best practices such as input validation, output encoding, and proper error handling, developers can significantly reduce the attack surface of their software applications. For example, input validation ensures that user inputs are rigorously checked and sanitized, effectively preventing common vulnerabilities like the SQL injection and Cross-Site Scripting (XSS) attacks. Proper error handling ensures that sensitive system details are not inadvertently exposed, making it far more challenging for attackers to exploit potential weaknesses.

Moreover, secure coding practices are indispensable in protecting sensitive data. In an era where data breaches and compromising confidential information are among the most significant cybersecurity concerns, secure coding practices serve as a protection against data breaches, especially within web applications. By employing robust encryption techniques for data both in transit and at rest, developers can ensure that sensitive information remains confidential and impervious to unauthorized access or interception. Secure coding practices shield user privacy and safeguard an organization's reputation and adherence to legal compliance.

Another compelling reason to champion secure coding practices is their role in preventing security incidents altogether. By rigorously adhering to established secure coding guidelines, developers proactively reduce the likelihood of vulnerabilities that malicious actors could exploit. This proactive approach helps organizations sidestep the severe consequences of security breaches, including financial losses, legal entanglements, and substantial damage to their reputation.

Beyond the technical aspects, secure coding practices contribute significantly to fostering trust and confidence in the digital realm. Trust is a linchpin in various domains, whether it's e-commerce, online banking, or healthcare services. Users must have unwavering faith that their data is handled securely and that their software applications are resilient against cyber threats. Secure coding practices shield users from harm and enhance their overall experience, cultivating trust and encouraging customer loyalty.

Furthermore, secure coding practices are indispensable for organizations striving to achieve and maintain regulatory compliance. Many industries are subject to stringent regulations concerning data protection and security. Secure coding practices provide the foundation for building and maintaining secure, compliant software systems, ensuring that organizations meet legal requirements and avoid the severe penalties and legal actions that non-compliance can entail.

Secure coding practices also lead to cost savings in the long term. By reducing the number of vulnerabilities in software applications, secure coding practices decrease the costs and effort required to identify and patch vulnerabilities after deployment. In essence, they offer an investment in security that pays dividends by minimizing the financial burden associated with vulnerability patching and enhancing the efficiency of development processes.

In conclusion, secure coding practices are not just a short-term solution; they are vital for the long-term sustainability of software systems. As cyber threats evolve and new vulnerabilities emerge, secure coding practices provide a robust defense against known and unknown risks. This adaptability ensures that software remains secure and resilient over time. In a world where software has become integral to our daily lives, secure coding practices are an indispensable aspect of delivering software applications that users can depend on—applications that protect their data, their privacy, and their trust.

CHAPTER IX

Network Security

Network security fundamentals

Network security is a paramount concern in today's hyperconnected world, where data flows seamlessly across networks and systems. For both individuals and organizations, maintaining the availability, confidentiality, and integrity of data and resources within a network is essential. This section explores the fundamental principles of network security, shedding light on the key concepts, strategies, and technologies that underpin this critical aspect of cybersecurity.

Confidentiality is one of the core tenets of network security. It ensures that data remains hidden from unauthorized access or disclosure. Encryption is a fundamental technique used to maintain confidentiality. Encryption safeguards sensitive information as it traverses the network by converting data into an unreadable cipher without the appropriate decryption key. Secure communication protocols like Transport Layer Security (TLS) and Virtual Private Networks (VPNs) employ encryption to establish confidential connections.

Data integrity ensures that information remains unaltered during transmission or storage. Hash functions play a pivotal role in maintaining data integrity. These functions generate a fixed-size hash value or checksum for a piece of data. By comparing the received hash value with the original one, recipients can verify if the data has been tampered with during transit. Additionally, digital signatures, which are generated using cryptographic techniques, help confirm the authenticity and integrity of data.

Availability in network security refers to the accessibility of data and resources when needed. DoS (Denial of Service) and Distributed Denial of Service (DDoS) attacks aim to disrupt the availability of network services. Network administrators employ load balancing, redundancy, and traffic filtering techniques to mitigate the impact of these attacks and ensure uninterrupted service availability.

Authentication is verifying the identity of users, devices, or systems attempting to access network resources. Secure authentication mechanisms, such as username-password pairs, biometrics, and multi-factor authentication (MFA), are used to confirm the legitimacy of users or devices. Robust authentication protocols are critical to preventing unauthorized access to sensitive data.

Authorization determines the level of access granted to authenticated users or devices. Access control lists (ACLs) and role-based access control (RBAC) are common authorization mechanisms. They specify what actions users or devices can perform and which resources they can access within the network.

Firewalls act as gatekeepers, examining incoming and outgoing network traffic to identify whether it should be allowed or blocked based on predefined security policies. Intrusion Detection Systems (IDS) complement firewalls by continuously monitoring network traffic for suspicious or malicious activities. IDS systems raise alerts when anomalies or potential threats are detected.

Virtual Private Networks (VPNs) establish secure, encrypted tunnels over public networks like the internet, allowing remote users or branch offices to connect to a corporate network securely. VPNs protect data in transit and ensure secure communication across untrusted networks.

Regularly applying patches and updates to network devices, operating systems, and software applications is essential. Vulnerabilities that are discovered and patched promptly reduce the risk of exploitation by attackers seeking to compromise network security.

Establishing comprehensive security policies and providing ongoing training for network administrators and users are fundamental aspects of network security. Security policies outline acceptable use, password management, and incident response procedures, while training ensures that individuals are aware of security best practices and can contribute to a secure network environment.

Continuous monitoring of network traffic and security events is necessary for detecting and responding to security incidents. Incident response plans define the actions to be taken when security breaches occur, enabling organizations to mitigate the impact and recover swiftly.

In conclusion, network security fundamentals encompass a range of principles and technologies that work together to protect data and resources' confidentiality, integrity, and availability within a network. Confidentiality and integrity are safeguarded through encryption and hash functions, while availability is maintained through strategies like load balancing and redundancy. Authentication and authorization mechanisms control access, while firewalls, IDS systems, and VPNs fortify the network perimeter. Patch management, security policies, and training contribute to a proactive defense, and security monitoring and incident response enable swift reactions to threats. In an era where information flows ceaselessly across networks, a strong foundation in network security is imperative to safeguarding the digital realm.

Firewall technologies and configurations

Firewalls are critical gatekeepers in network security, providing the first line of defense against unauthorized access and cyber threats. These security devices, whether implemented as hardware appliances or software solutions, are a barrier between trusted internal networks and untrusted external networks, like the internet. This section explores firewall technologies and configurations, highlighting their essential role in safeguarding network perimeters and data.

Packet filtering firewalls are the most fundamental type of firewalls. They operate at the OSI model's network layer (Layer 3), examining incoming and outgoing packets based on predefined rules. These rules determine whether a packet should be allowed or denied based on criteria like source IP address, destination IP address, and port numbers. Packet filtering firewalls are efficient and suitable for simple network architectures but lack the sophistication to inspect packet contents, making them vulnerable to certain types of attacks.

Stateful inspection firewalls, or dynamic packet filtering firewalls, offer enhanced security compared to packet filtering firewalls. They maintain a state table that tracks the state of active connections, allowing them to make context-aware decisions. This means they can evaluate the state of a connection and allow return traffic that is part of an established connection, improving security and reducing the risk of particular types of attacks. Stateful inspection firewalls are effective for many network configurations but may struggle with more complex protocols and applications.

Proxy firewalls operate at the OSI model's application layer (Layer 7). They act as intermediaries between clients and servers, receiving and forwarding requests on behalf of clients. This enables them to inspect and filter application-layer traffic, making them highly effective at detecting and preventing application-layer attacks, such as those targeting web applications. Proxy firewalls, however, may introduce latency due to the extra processing involved, and they require specific proxy configurations for different applications.

Next-Generation Firewalls (NGFWs) combine traditional firewall functionality with advanced features, like intrusion prevention systems (IPS), application-layer filtering, and deep packet inspection (DPI). NGFWs go beyond the traditional port and protocol-based filtering of earlier firewalls, allowing them to identify and block specific applications and even recognize and filter content within those applications. They provide a more comprehensive defense against modern threats but require higher configuration and management.

Unified Threat Management (UTM) Firewalls are all-in-one security solutions that combine various security features, including firewalling, intrusion detection and prevention, antivirus, anti-spam, and content filtering. These devices make managing network security easier by combining several security features into a single appliance or software program. UTM firewalls are particularly useful for small- to medium-sized businesses seeking an integrated, easy-to-manage security solution.

Configuring a firewall effectively is crucial to its performance and security. Security policies should be defined to specify what traffic is allowed or denied. These policies are based on rules that take application protocols, port numbers, and source and destination IP addresses into account. Additionally, firewall administrators must keep the rule set up-to-date, regularly reviewing and adjusting it to align with evolving security requirements.

In conclusion, firewall technologies and configurations are pivotal in safeguarding network perimeters and data from unauthorized access and cyber threats. Different types of firewalls, from basic packet filtering to sophisticated NGFWs and UTM firewalls, offer various levels of protection and flexibility. The choice of firewall technology depends on an organization's specific security requirements and network complexity. Proper configuration and ongoing management are essential to ensure that firewalls effectively fulfill their role as gatekeepers, enabling organizations to maintain their networks' and data's security and integrity in an increasingly interconnected digital landscape.

Intrusion detection and prevention in network security

Intrusion detection and prevention systems (IDPS) are foundational components of network security, serving as vigilant guardians against cyber threats. They are pivotal in monitoring network traffic for suspicious activities and responding proactively to potential threats. IDPS solutions are indispensable in safeguarding network assets, data, and the overall integrity of digital operations. This section delves into the critical significance of intrusion detection and prevention in network security, elucidating their fundamental concepts, methodologies, and practical applications.

Intrusion Detection Systems (IDS) are the initial line of defense in the realm of IDPS. Their primary function is to identify and alert network administrators to any suspicious or malicious activities occurring within a network. These activities could encompass unauthorized access attempts, deviations in network traffic patterns, or the recognition of known attack signatures. IDS operates through two primary methodologies: signature-based detection and anomaly-based detection.

Signature-based detection, also known as rule-based IDS, relies on a database of predefined attack signatures or patterns. When network traffic matches a known signature, the IDS generates an alert. While signature-based IDS effectively identifies known threats, it may struggle to detect novel or sophisticated attacks that do not align with established patterns.

Anomaly-based detection, on the other hand, establishes a baseline of normal network behavior and continuously monitors for deviations from this baseline. When significant deviations are detected, the IDS generates an alert. Anomaly-based IDS is invaluable for identifying previously unseen attacks but can produce false positives if the baseline is not accurately defined or legitimate network behavior changes are misinterpreted.

Intrusion Prevention Systems (IPS) build upon the capabilities of IDS by actively blocking or mitigating malicious activities in real-time. IPS uses the same detection methodologies as IDS (signature-based and anomaly-based) but incorporates mechanisms for immediate action, such as blocking suspicious traffic or resetting connections. This proactive approach ensures that threats are addressed promptly and effectively.

IDPS is of paramount importance in network security for several compelling reasons. Firstly, it enables the timely detection of suspicious activities, empowering network administrators to respond swiftly to potential threats before they escalate. Secondly, IDPS minimizes network downtime and disruptions to critical operations by identifying and mitigating threats in real-time. Moreover, signature-based detection effectively safeguards against known attack patterns, providing organizations robust protection against well-documented threats. Finally, anomaly-based detection offers the adaptability needed to identify new and previously unseen attacks, flagging deviations from baseline behavior.

In practical terms, IDPS finds application in various real-world scenarios to protect networked systems. Enterprises deploy IDPS in their corporate networks to safeguard sensitive data, prevent data breaches, and ensure the uninterrupted operation of critical business systems. Critical infrastructure sectors, including energy, transportation, and healthcare, rely on IDPS to protect against cyberattacks that could have catastrophic consequences. Cloud service providers use IDPS to secure their infrastructure and safeguard customer data and applications hosted in the cloud. E-commerce platforms and financial institutions employ IDPS to secure transactions, protect customer data, and safeguard financial assets from cyber threats.

In conclusion, systems for detecting and preventing intrusions are the vigilant defenders of network security; they constantly monitor network traffic for indications of malicious or suspicious activities. With their ability to detect known and emerging threats, IDPS plays a crucial role in safeguarding networked systems, reducing downtime, and protecting sensitive data. As cyber threats evolve, intrusion detection and prevention remain essential components of a comprehensive network security strategy, helping organizations stay resilient and secure in the face of an ever-changing threat landscape.

Securing wireless networks

In our modern, hyperconnected world, wireless networks have become an integral part of our daily lives, offering us the convenience and flexibility to access the internet and corporate resources from virtually anywhere. However, this convenience comes with its own set of security challenges, making the need to secure wireless networks paramount. The security of wireless networks is not just about protecting sensitive data but also about ensuring the confidentiality of communications and preventing unauthorized access. This section will delve into the significance of securing wireless networks and explore key strategies and technologies to mitigate security risks effectively.

Encryption serves as one of the foundational principles of wireless network security. It is essential for converting data into a format that is unreadable that requires the right decryption key to be deciphered. Strong encryption protocols, such as Wi-Fi Protected Access 3 (WPA3) for Wi-Fi networks, ensure that data transmitted between devices and access points remains confidential and secure. Encryption is a critical safeguard that prevents eavesdropping and thwarts any attempts to intercept sensitive information.

Another crucial aspect of securing wireless networks is the implementation of robust authentication mechanisms. It is crucial to make sure that these networks are only accessible to authorized users. Robust authentication methods, such as WPA3-Enterprise, require users to authenticate with unique credentials, including usernames and passwords, digital certificates, or even multi-factor authentication (MFA). Multi-factor authentication, in particular, adds an extra layer of security by mandating users to provide multiple forms of verification, making it significantly more challenging for unauthorized individuals to gain access.

Strong passwords are a fundamental part of wireless network security. The strength of the passwords used to access wireless networks and associated devices is paramount. Weak or easily guessable passwords can be exploited by attackers, potentially leading to network breaches. To mitigate this risk, network administrators should enforce stringent password policies encouraging users to create complex and unique passwords and mandate regular password changes. Passphrase-based authentication, which combines several words into a single, lengthy password, is one way to enhance password security.

Network segmentation is another strategy that enhances the security of wireless networks. Network segmentation reduces the attack surface by isolating different parts of the network. For instance, organizations often create separate guest networks that are isolated from their internal corporate networks, ensuring that guest devices do not have direct access to sensitive resources. This practice helps maintain network security by limiting the exposure of critical assets to potential threats.

Regularly updating firmware and software on wireless devices, including routers and access points, is critical in maintaining wireless network security. Updates which address security vulnerabilities and enhance network security generally are often released by manufacturers. Effective patch management ensures that known vulnerabilities are addressed promptly, significantly reducing the risk of exploitation by attackers who seek to exploit known weaknesses.

Intrusion detection and prevention systems, or IDPS are essential tools for monitoring wireless network traffic for suspicious activities and potential threats. These systems analyze network packets, detect anomalies, and raise alerts when unusual behavior is detected. IDPS can block malicious traffic and help maintain the integrity of the network by determining and mitigating threats in real-time.

Physical security measures should not be overlooked in the context of wireless network security. Access points and network infrastructure should be placed securely to prevent physical tampering or theft. Organizations should also implement measures to prevent unauthorized physical access to network devices, which can serve as potential entry points for attackers.

Wireless Intrusion Detection Systems (WIDS) are specialized systems designed to monitor and secure wireless networks. They can detect rogue access points, unauthorized clients, and other wireless security threats. WIDS complements traditional network security measures, providing visibility and control over wireless network activity, and enabling organizations to respond proactively to wireless security incidents.

Finally, security awareness and training play a vital role in ensuring the security of wireless networks. Educating users and IT staff about wireless security best practices is essential. Users should be aware of the risks of connecting to public Wi-Fi networks and be cautious when sharing sensitive information over wireless connections. IT staff should receive training on configuring and maintaining secure wireless networks and staying updated on emerging threats and security best practices.

In conclusion, securing wireless networks is imperative in our digitally interconnected world. While wireless networks offer unprecedented convenience and mobility, they also present security challenges that must be addressed comprehensively. Encryption, strong authentication, secure passwords, network segmentation, firmware updates, intrusion detection, physical security, and the use of specialized systems like WIDS are all critical components of a robust wireless network security strategy. By implementing these measures and fostering a culture of security awareness, organizations can protect sensitive data, maintain the confidentiality of communications, and ensure that wireless networks remain a secure and reliable means of connectivity in an increasingly digital landscape.

CHAPTER X

Emerging Trends in Cybersecurity and Ethical Hacking

AI and machine learning in cybersecurity

Artificial Intelligence (AI) and Machine Learning (ML) have ushered in a new era in the field of cybersecurity, where the dynamic and evolving nature of cyber threats necessitates innovative approaches to defense. These technologies have proven to be invaluable assets in strengthening cybersecurity by augmenting the capabilities of human analysts and traditional security systems. Their transformative impact is evident across various facets of cybersecurity, from threat detection and predictive analysis to behavioral analysis, phishing detection, and malware mitigation.

AI and ML excel in threat detection by harnessing their pattern recognition capabilities. They scrutinize vast datasets of network traffic, user behavior, and system logs, identifying subtle anomalies that may signal a cyberattack. Continually learning from historical data, these systems adapt to emerging threats, enhancing their ability to detect new and previously unseen dangers. Predictive analysis is another powerful application, enabling organizations to anticipate threats by analyzing historical data and trends. Being proactive in addressing vulnerabilities before they can be exploited is made possible by this foresight.

Behavioral analysis, bolstered by AI and ML, revolutionizes user authentication and access control.

These technologies monitor and learn from users' typical behavior, recognizing anomalies that may indicate unauthorized access attempts. This dynamic authentication method surpasses traditional, static approaches like passwords, which are susceptible to breaches. Moreover, in the ongoing battle against phishing attacks, AI-driven solutions evaluate email content, URLs, and sender behavior, promptly recognizing suspicious patterns to thwart phishing attempts.

AI and ML have significantly enhanced malware detection and mitigation. To identify malicious code, machine learning algorithms analyze file behavior, network traffic, and system activity. Endpoint protection solutions empowered by AI can isolate infected devices, preventing malware from spreading through networks. Automated incident response is yet another invaluable application. AI and ML can assess the scope and severity of an incident, suggest remediation actions, and even initiate automated responses, facilitating swift reactions to security incidents.

These technologies further contribute to cybersecurity by automating threat intelligence and data analysis. AI can efficiently process vast volumes of threat intelligence data, correlating information from multiple sources to identify emerging threats and track threat actors. Such intelligence empowers organizations with actionable insights to strengthen their security posture. Vulnerability management also benefits from AI and ML, with these technologies prioritizing vulnerabilities based on their potential impact and likelihood of exploitation. This data-driven approach enables efficient resource allocation for patching or mitigating the most critical vulnerabilities.

In network security and traffic analysis, AI-driven solutions offer real-time monitoring capabilities. These systems can dynamically identify and respond to suspicious activities, intrusions, and malware infections.

They adapt to evolving network conditions and scale to handle the extensive volume of data generated by modern networks.

In conclusion, AI and ML have revolutionized cybersecurity by augmenting human capabilities and traditional security systems. Their prowess in detecting threats, predicting attacks, and automating responses has made them indispensable in defending against an ever-evolving cyber threat landscape. As cyberattacks become more sophisticated, AI and ML-driven cybersecurity solutions provide a proactive and adaptive defense, helping organizations and individuals stay ahead of adversaries and protect their digital assets. With the continued advancement of AI and ML technologies, the future of cybersecurity promises to be even more resilient and effective in safeguarding the digital realm.

IoT security challenges

The Internet of Things (IoT) rapid expansion has heralded a new era of connectivity and automation, reshaping the way we live and work. From wearable devices and smart homes to industrial sensors and autonomous vehicles, the Internet of Things has impacted many aspects of our lives. However, this unprecedented proliferation of IoT devices has brought with it a multitude of security challenges that pose significant risks to individuals, organizations, and critical infrastructure.

First and foremost, IoT devices' sheer diversity and volume present a considerable challenge. These devices, from everyday household appliances to complex industrial sensors, have unique capabilities and vulnerabilities. Managing the security of this vast ecosystem is a intricate task that requires a comprehensive approach.

Furthermore, many IoT devices suffer from inadequate authentication and authorization mechanisms. Attackers often exploit weak or default credentials to gain unauthorized access. Without robust authentication and proper authorization, malicious actors can manipulate IoT devices for their gain.

Another critical concern is the vulnerability of IoT devices' firmware and software. Manufacturers may not prioritize regular security updates and patches, exposing these devices to known exploits. Consequently, IoT devices can become entry points for cyberattacks on more extensive networks.

Data privacy and encryption also remain significant challenges in the IoT landscape. IoT devices gather and transmit vast amounts of data, including sensitive and personally identifiable information. Inadequate data privacy measures and encryption mechanisms can lead to data breaches, potentially violating privacy regulations and exposing individuals to harm.

Lack of standardization further complicates IoT security efforts. The absence of standardized security protocols and practices across the IoT ecosystem creates interoperability issues and vulnerabilities that attackers can exploit.

Resource constraints, like limited processing power and memory in many IoT devices, hinder the implementation of robust security features. This limitation can make it challenging to deploy security patches and updates promptly.

Physical security is another concern, as IoT devices can be physically accessible to attackers. In situations where physical access is gained, devices can be tampered with or replaced with malicious counterparts, posing significant security risks.

IoT device security threats can arise at any point in the device's long and intricate global supply chain, from production to distribution. Attackers might release compromised devices onto the market by taking advantage of vulnerabilities in the supply chain.

Lack of awareness and education regarding IoT security is a pervasive issue. Many consumers and even some organizations may not be fully aware of the security risks associated with IoT devices. This lack of awareness can result in poor security practices, such as failing to change default passwords or neglecting to update firmware.

Lastly, the complexity of IoT ecosystems, which consist of a multitude of devices, networks, and cloud services, adds another layer of complexity to security efforts. Securing this intricate web of interactions, where data flows between devices and services, necessitates a comprehensive and coordinated approach to security.

Addressing these IoT security challenges is essential to ensure IoT technology's continued growth and integration into our lives and critical infrastructure. Stakeholders, including device manufacturers, service providers, regulatory bodies, and end-users, must collaborate to establish security best practices, standards, and regulations. Manufacturers must prioritize security by designing devices with built-in security features, providing regular updates and patches, and educating users about security practices. End-users must remain vigilant about securing their IoT devices, changing default passwords, and keeping firmware up to date.

In conclusion, while IoT has unlocked unprecedented opportunities for connectivity and automation, it has also ushered in a host of security challenges. The complex and diverse nature of IoT devices and vulnerabilities in authentication, authorization, firmware, and supply chains present a fertile ground for cyber threats. To fully realize the potential of IoT while safeguarding against these threats, a concerted effort to address these challenges is imperative. By implementing robust security measures, fostering awareness, and establishing industry-wide standards, we can create a more secure and resilient IoT ecosystem that benefits individuals, organizations, and society.

Blockchain and cybersecurity

Blockchain technology, designed initially to underpin cryptocurrencies like Bitcoin, has evolved to find applications across various industries. One of the most promising and impactful domains where blockchain has demonstrated its potential is cybersecurity. Blockchain's inherent properties, such as decentralization, immutability, transparency, and cryptographic security, make it a powerful tool for bolstering cybersecurity efforts. This section will explore the symbiotic relationship between blockchain and cybersecurity, examining how blockchain is revolutionizing security practices and addressing key challenges in the digital landscape.

Blockchain is fundamentally a dispersed network of computers that maintains a decentralized ledger of transactions. Each new transaction is added to a chain of existing transactions, creating a tamper-resistant and transparent history of events. The immutability of blockchain ensures that once a transaction is recorded, it cannot be altered or deleted, making it an ideal technology for maintaining the integrity of data and records.

One of blockchain's fundamental contributions to cybersecurity is enhancing data integrity. Traditional centralized systems are vulnerable to data manipulation and breaches, as they rely on a single point of control. In contrast, blockchain's decentralized nature ensures that data stored on the network cannot be altered without consensus from most participants. This property makes it exceptionally difficult for attackers to tamper with or manipulate data stored on a blockchain.

Blockchain also offers robust authentication and identity management solutions. With the growth of identity theft and data breaches, traditional authentication methods have proven inadequate. Blockchain's cryptographic capabilities enable the creation of secure digital identities. Users can have a unique and verifiable digital identity stored on a blockchain, which they can use to authenticate themselves securely without relying on centralized identity providers.

The technology has further revolutionized access control and authorization mechanisms. Contracts that are self-executing and have their terms encoded directly into code, known as smart contracts, enable automated and transparent access control. These contracts can be employed to define and enforce access permissions and data-sharing agreements, reducing the risk of unauthorized access to sensitive information.

Blockchain's role in cybersecurity extends to secure communications and data sharing. Blockchain networks can facilitate secure peer-to-peer communications and data exchange by leveraging encryption techniques and decentralized storage. This is particularly relevant in industries including finance and healthcare, where the security and privacy of data are paramount.

In the realm of threat detection and response, blockchain can enhance cybersecurity practices by providing an immutable record of network activity. Any changes or anomalies in network behavior can be quickly identified and investigated, as blockchain records can be used to reconstruct the history of events leading up to a security incident.

While blockchain offers several significant advantages in cybersecurity, it has challenges and limitations. Scalability issues, energy consumption, and regulatory concerns are among the key challenges that must be addressed as blockchain evolves in the cybersecurity landscape. Additionally, the adoption of blockchain technologies in mainstream cybersecurity practices is still in its early stages, requiring further development and integration.

In conclusion, blockchain technology has appeared as a potent ally in the fight against cyber threats. Its decentralized and immutable nature enhances data integrity, authentication, access control, secure communications, and threat detection. Blockchain is proving to be an essential tool in safeguarding digital assets, mitigating risks, and protecting sensitive information in an increasingly interconnected and digital world. As the technology continues to mature and adapt, it is poised to play an even more pivotal role in shaping cybersecurity's future. However, it is crucial to recognize that blockchain is not a panacea; it is a tool that can significantly bolster our cybersecurity defenses when applied thoughtfully and strategically.

The future of ethical hacking

Ethical hacking, often called penetration testing or white-hat hacking, has established itself as a critical pillar of cybersecurity in our increasingly digital world. These cybersecurity professionals leverage their skills and expertise to uncover vulnerabilities and weaknesses in computer systems, networks, and applications. As we peer into the future, the domain of ethical hacking promises to be both thrilling and challenging, driven by several transformative factors and emerging trends.

First and foremost, the ever-evolving cyber threat landscape demands that ethical hackers continuously adapt and evolve their skill sets. Cyber attackers are becoming increasingly sophisticated, employing advanced techniques and technologies. Ethical hackers must deeply understand emerging threats, including those tied to artificial intelligence (AI), the Internet of Things (IoT), and quantum computing. Staying ahead of these malicious actors will require ongoing education and a proactive approach.

AI as well as machine learning are revolutionizing cybersecurity. Ethical hackers are increasingly incorporating AI-driven tools and techniques into their arsenals. These technologies facilitate automation in vulnerability assessments, anomaly detection in network traffic, and the analysis of vast datasets for security insights. Ethical hacking in the future will see a greater reliance on AI for both offensive and defensive purposes.

The proliferation of IoT devices is introducing new security challenges. Ethical hackers will play a pivotal role in identifying vulnerabilities within IoT ecosystems, encompassing everything from smart homes and wearable gadgets to industrial sensors and autonomous vehicles. Safeguarding these interconnected devices will become a top priority for organizations, with ethical hackers as key contributors.

Quantum computing, while holding immense promise, also poses a significant threat to existing encryption algorithms. Ethical hackers will be at the forefront of efforts to develop and test quantum-resistant encryption methods to protect sensitive data. Furthermore, quantum computing offers ethical hackers new tools and opportunities to explore vulnerabilities and develop more secure cryptographic systems.

Data protection regulations, like GDPR and CCPA, are becoming increasingly stringent, imposing strict requirements on organizations to safeguard user data. Ethical hackers will become essential partners in helping organizations comply with these regulations. They will identify and address security gaps to ensure data privacy and protection.

Bug bounty programs, which reward ethical hackers for responsibly disclosing vulnerabilities, are becoming more widespread. Organizations recognize the value of crowdsourced security testing and will expand their bug bounty initiatives. Ethical hackers will have more opportunities to contribute to the security of widely used software and platforms.

The requirement for ethical hackers will continue to surge, leading to the field's professionalization. Ethical hacking certifications, such as Certified Ethical Hacker (CEH) and Offensive Security Certified Professional (OSCP), will gain further recognition and respect within the industry.

Collaboration and information sharing will be essential to the future ethical hacking landscape. Ethical hackers will increasingly collaborate with peers, security researchers, and organizations to share knowledge and insights about emerging threats and vulnerabilities. This collaborative approach will be critical in staying ahead of cybercriminals.

The shift to cloud computing presents both opportunities and challenges for ethical hackers. As organizations migrate their data and services to the cloud, ethical hackers must focus on assessing cloud security configurations, identifying misconfigurations, and ensuring the protection of cloud-based assets.

In the realm of education, ethical hacking instruction will become more accessible and comprehensive. Online courses, workshops, and certification programs will empower individuals to expand the skills and knowledge required to become ethical hackers.

In conclusion, the future of ethical hacking is characterized by dynamic change and exciting opportunities. Ethical hackers will continue to play a pivotal role in defending against evolving cyber threats, securing IoT ecosystems, addressing quantum computing challenges, and ensuring regulatory compliance. Collaboration, continuous learning, and the adoption of cutting-edge technologies will be central to the success of ethical hackers in this ever-changing landscape. As organizations increasingly recognize the importance of proactive security measures, ethical hackers will remain at the forefront of safeguarding digital assets and protecting sensitive information. The future of ethical hacking promises to be a vital and thriving field in the ongoing battle against cyber threats.

CONCLUSION

Summarizing the key takeaways

This book, titled "Guardians of the Virtual Realm: From Protection to Penetration - Navigating Cybersecurity and Ethical Hacking Techniques," has taken readers on a comprehensive journey through the realms of cybersecurity and ethical hacking. As we conclude our exploration, we must recap the key takeaways and insights gained from this extensive guide.

First and foremost, the book highlighted the critical importance of cybersecurity in today's digital landscape. With the increasing reliance on technology and the escalating frequency and sophistication of cyber threats, organizations and individuals alike must prioritize cybersecurity as a fundamental aspect of their operations and daily lives. It's no longer a matter of if, but when, a cyber threat will be encountered, underscoring the need for proactive cybersecurity measures.

The book delved into the concept of cybersecurity, explaining its fundamental principles and the triad of key components: threats, vulnerabilities, and risks. Understanding these elements is essential for crafting an effective cybersecurity strategy. Threats encompass a wide range of potential attacks, while vulnerabilities are the weaknesses that threat actors exploit. The interplay between these factors defines the level of risk an organization faces, emphasizing the need for risk assessment and mitigation.

One of the central themes explored in this book is the significance of ethical hacking or penetration testing. Ethical hackers, also known as white-hat hackers, play a crucial role in determining and addressing vulnerabilities before malicious actors can exploit them. By embracing ethical hacking as a proactive approach to cybersecurity, organizations can bolster their defenses, ensuring that their systems and data remain secure.

The book also delved into the ethics and legality surrounding hacking activities. It emphasized the importance of conducting ethical hacking within the boundaries of the law and with proper authorization. Ethical hackers must adhere to strict ethical guidelines and respect privacy and confidentiality while carrying out their duties.

A key distinction highlighted in this book is the differentiation between ethical hackers and malicious hackers. While both groups possess similar technical skills, their intentions and actions set them apart. Ethical hackers work to strengthen cybersecurity by identifying vulnerabilities and reporting them to the appropriate authorities for remediation. In contrast, malicious hackers engage in cybercrime for personal gain or to cause harm, making them a significant threat to organizations and individuals.

The significance of penetration testing, a core element of ethical hacking, was underscored in this book. Penetration testing allows organizations to simulate real-world cyberattacks, enabling them to identify weaknesses and vulnerabilities in their systems and processes. Organizations can proactively address vulnerabilities and enhance their cybersecurity posture by conducting regular penetration tests.

The book also provided insights into current cyber threats, discussing various types of cyberattacks such as phishing, malware, and distributed denial of service attacks. Real-world examples of major cyber incidents were presented, highlighting the devastating impact these attacks can have on organizations, including financial losses and reputational damage. Understanding these threats and their consequences is crucial for organizations seeking to defend against them effectively.

Lastly, the book explored essential cybersecurity tools and technologies, including antivirus software, intrusion detection and prevention systems, firewalls, as well as security information and event management systems. These tools are critical components of a robust cybersecurity infrastructure, helping organizations detect, prevent, and respond to cyber threats effectively.

In conclusion, this book has provided a comprehensive overview of cybersecurity and ethical hacking, offering readers valuable insights into the evolving world of digital security. The key takeaways from this journey emphasize the need for proactive cybersecurity measures, ethical hacking to enhance security, the importance of adherence to ethical and legal standards, and the critical role of penetration testing and cybersecurity tools. As we navigate the ever-changing digital landscape, staying informed and vigilant is paramount in protecting digital assets and data.

Encouraging continuous learning and adaptation in the field

The importance of continuous learning and adaptation cannot be overstated in the fast-paced and ever-evolving realm of cybersecurity and ethical hacking. The digital landscape is in a perpetual state of flux, with cyber threats growing in complexity and frequency. To stay ahead of malicious actors and effectively safeguard digital assets, professionals in the field must embrace a mindset of lifelong learning and adaptability.

One of the core tenets of cybersecurity is the understanding that the landscape is constantly changing. New vulnerabilities emerge, innovative attack vectors are devised, and cybercriminals continually refine their tactics. Professionals must regularly update their knowledge and skills to counteract these evolving threats. This means staying current with the latest cybersecurity trends, tools, and techniques. It also involves regularly attending industry conferences, webinars, and workshops to gain insights from experts and peers.

Certifications are a valuable means of formalizing one's expertise and staying updated with the latest industry standards. Leading certifications such as Certified Information Systems Security Professional (or CISSP), Certified Ethical Hacker (CEH), and Certified Information Security Manager (CISM) provide structured curricula and assessments that ensure professionals are well-versed in the latest cybersecurity practices. Pursuing these certifications enhances one's knowledge and demonstrates a commitment to maintaining the highest criterias of cybersecurity.

The world of ethical hacking, a crucial component of cybersecurity, is no exception to the need for continuous learning. Ethical hackers, also known as white-hat hackers, identify and mitigate vulnerabilities before malicious actors can exploit them. To excel in this role, ethical hackers must remain on the cutting edge of cybersecurity, continually honing their skills in penetration testing, vulnerability assessment, and network security. Recognized certifications like Certified Ethical Hacker (CEH) and Offensive Security Certified Professional (OSCP) validate the expertise of ethical hackers, emphasizing the importance of ongoing training.

In addition to formal education and certification, informal learning plays a pivotal role in the field. Cybersecurity communities and forums provide invaluable platforms for professionals to share knowledge, discuss emerging threats, and seek advice. Online platforms like cybersecurity-focused blogs, podcasts, and YouTube channels offer accessible and up-to-date information on various topics within the field. Professionals should actively engage with these resources to broaden their understanding and sharpen their skills.

Cybersecurity professionals should also embrace a proactive approach to adaptation. This involves anticipating emerging threats and vulnerabilities rather than merely responding to known issues. Threat intelligence, which requires monitoring and analyzing cyber threats and vulnerabilities, is critical to this approach. By staying informed about the most current threats and attack techniques, professionals can better prepare their organizations and take proactive measures to prevent security breaches.

Furthermore, adopting emerging technologies such as artificial intelligence (AI) and machine learning (ML) has become integral to cybersecurity. These technologies can potentially automate threat detection and response, providing a more proactive and adaptive defense. Professionals must familiarize themselves with AI and ML tools and techniques to harness their potential effectively.

In conclusion, continuous learning and adaptation are essential principles for success in the dynamic field of cybersecurity and ethical hacking. Professionals who prioritize ongoing education, pursue certifications, engage with the cybersecurity community, and proactively anticipate threats are better equipped to fight against evolving cyber threats. In a landscape where digital security is paramount, the commitment to lifelong learning and adaptability is not just a choice but a necessity to effectively protect digital assets and data.

Emphasizing the importance of cybersecurity in the digital era

In the digital era, where nearly every aspect of our personal and professional lives is intertwined with technology, the importance of cybersecurity has never been more pronounced. Our reliance on digital systems for communication, commerce, healthcare, education, and entertainment has made us more vulnerable than ever to cyber threats. Everyone is a potential target, from individuals to small businesses to large corporations and governments. Emphasizing the importance of cybersecurity is not just a matter of safeguarding data; it's about protecting our way of life in this interconnected world.

First and foremost, cybersecurity is critical for safeguarding sensitive data. Our personal and financial information, intellectual property, medical records, and more are stored digitally. Cyberattacks can result in the theft or compromise of this data, leading to identity theft, financial losses, and privacy violations. Organizations, in particular, have a duty to protect the data of their customers and clients. Legal repercussions and reputational damage are possible outcomes of data breaches. Hence, robust cybersecurity measures are essential to prevent unauthorized access and data breaches.

Moreover, cybersecurity plays a pivotal role in ensuring the integrity of digital systems. It is not just about protecting data from theft but also about guaranteeing that the data has not been tampered with. For instance, in critical sectors like healthcare and finance, the accuracy and integrity of data are paramount. Any unauthorized changes to patient records or financial transactions can have severe consequences. Cybersecurity measures like data encryption and digital signatures help maintain data integrity, assuring users that the information they access or transmit is reliable and unaltered.

Cybersecurity is vital for national security in the digital era, where information is shared globally. Governments rely on interconnected systems for defense, infrastructure, and communication. Cyberattacks can disrupt these critical functions, potentially compromising the security of a nation. State-sponsored cyberattacks are a growing concern, with countries using cyber warfare tactics to steal sensitive information, disrupt services, and even disable critical infrastructure. This underscores the need for robust cybersecurity strategies to protect national interests and security.

The digital economy is another area where cybersecurity plays a pivotal role. E-commerce, online banking, and digital payment systems have revolutionized how we conduct business. However, they have also become attractive targets for cybercriminals seeking financial gain. Without effective cybersecurity measures, the trust and confidence of consumers in digital transactions can erode, hindering the growth of the digital economy. Organizations must invest in secure online platforms and payment gateways to protect their customers and foster a safe and thriving digital marketplace.

Education and awareness about cybersecurity are essential in the digital era. Many cyber threats exploit human vulnerabilities through tactics like phishing, social engineering, and ransomware attacks. Individuals and employees in organizations must be educated about these threats and how to recognize and respond to them. Training programs and awareness campaigns can empower individuals to take proactive steps in protecting their digital lives, from using strong passwords to practicing safe online behaviors.

In conclusion, emphasizing the importance of cybersecurity in the digital era is not an option but a necessity. It is essential for safeguarding sensitive data, ensuring data integrity, protecting national security, enabling the digital economy, and empowering individuals with the knowledge to defend against cyber threats. With the development of technology comes the sophistication of cyber threats, the commitment to robust cybersecurity measures must be unwavering. In an interconnected world, the security of our digital systems and the protection of our way of life depend on it.

Thank you for buying and reading/listening to our book. If you found this book useful/helpful please take a few minutes and leave a review on the platform where you purchased our book. Your feedback matters greatly to us.